Alaska Flyfishing:
The Call of the River
by Dan Heiner

Spend A Season Fly-fishing Alaska
with Outdoor Writer Dan Heiner
as he Experiences Several of The Last Frontier's
Premier Waters

FLY-FISHING ALASKA

ISBN 0-9637407-8-4

Cover Photo of Alagnak River Rainbow Trout
Caught and Released by Tony Sarp
Photo by Trey Combs

-Published by-
Dan Heiner's •FISHING ALASKA ™
205 East Dimond Blvd. #100
Anchorage, Alaska 99515

Alaska Flyfishing:

THE CALL OF THE RIVER ©

is a copyrighted title.

Dan Heiner's • FISHING ALASKA ™
is a Registered Trademark
and a Licensed Alaska Business

Photographs Not Otherwise Credited
Were Taken By The Author

Manufactured in the United States of America

Word Processing Assistance: David Stark
Photo Credits Where Applicable
Layout/Format: Dan Heiner
Title by Author

Illustrations by Karol Fogel
and Melody Blevins

Dan Heiner's Articles Have Appeared In:

Flyfishing magazine
Salmon Trout Steelheader magazine
SAFARI magazine
Alaska Outdoors magazine
Alaska Outdoor Times

ISBN 0-9637407-8-4

Dedication -

This book is dedicated to
Dr. Leon "Joe" Chandler,

Lester Jacober,

and Bernie and John Ortman, Jr.,

who, in their own, inimitable styles
epitomize the spirit of fly-fishing in Alaska.

It is also dedicated to all those
Alaska guides, owners, lodges, and services
who, over the past several years
have invited the author to accompany them
to many of Alaska's premier waters.

Dan Heiner

The Fascination of Flyfishing

Lies In The Fact
That Nobody Can Predict
Just When or What Might Happen

- On Any Given Cast.

- Annonymous

Follow Your Dream...

Until one is committed there is hesitancy, the chance to draw back, always ineffectiveness. Concerning all acts of initiative (and creation), there is one elementary truth, the ignorance of which kills countless ideas and splendid plans: That the moment one definitely commits oneself, then Providence moves *too*.

All sorts of things occur to help one that would never otherwise have occurred. A whole stream of events issues from the decision, raising in one's favor all manner of unforeseen incidents and meetings and material assistance, which no man could have dreamt would have come his way.

I have learned a deep respect for one of Goethe's couplets: Whatever you can do or dream you can...

Begin It.

Boldness has genius, power, and magic in it.

W. H. Murray

Acknowledgments

The author would like to thank the following people:

My wife, Anne Heiner, for her patience
and understanding of this undertaking

-and-

Paul D. Rotkis
Tom Coomer
John Swett
Bob Johnson
Willy Morris
John Staser
Harry Geron, Tackle Advisor
David Stark, Word Processing
Sue Ohrberg, The CopyWright
Evan Swensen, for the start
Vera Clair for all
Nanci Morris
Trey Combs
Nick Amato
G. Loomis, Inc.

With Special Thanks To My Father
Daniel P. Heiner,
My Favorite Fishing Partner

Table of Contents

Introduction
by Nanci Morris
Alaska Fly-fishing Guide

In this book you are invited to spend a season fly-fishing Alaska with outdoor writer Dan Heiner. That's exciting to me, because when I stop and think about it, I realize it is because of people like Dan that our imaginary worlds become a reality.

Because I make my living guiding fly-fishers in Alaska, amongst the wonders of nature, I can truly appreciate what Dan has given to the sport through his writings. I am confidant that once you have absorbed the spirit of this work you will discover much more to appreciate about the wonderful world of fly-fishing – and all that goes with it. As you will see, Dan takes his fishing seriously, but not too seriously, like some people do. To Dan, fly-fishing is a sport which, above all else, offers people a chance to intimately share and experience the wonders of the outdoors, and for the past dozen years Dan has chosen the wild rivers of Alaska as his setting. His passion for experiencing Alaska's rivers is exceeded by no one.

Dan understands that there are elements in the world of fly-fishing that contain unmistakable grace and beauty; elements such as a fresh, clear mountain stream that succumbs each year to the icy hand of winter, only to appear again in spring, renewing its promise to the land and the fish within – to an intricate, painstakingly-fashioned, hand-tied fly, a creation which suddenly seems to take on a soul and character all of its own.

Dan has taken the time to put these elements into print, something you and I always promise to do ... someday... but somehow never seem to get around to doing.

The characters in this book are all real people. This is Dan's Alaska – up close and personal – with its varied, wild rivers, its powerful fish, and its array of extremely colorful individuals.

Because Dan appreciates the quiet, intrinsic beauty and friendly camaraderie associated with fly-fishing as much as he does the action of battling fish, he is able to take you along with him to the wonderous places he has visited, allowing you to share in his Alaska dream.

The places mentioned in this book are also real; remote lakes, rivers, and Alaska fly-fishing lodges that many of you will experience only through Dan's words. Others of you, however, will reach out and grasp the spirit and adventure of fly-fishing Alaska as Dan describes it, embarking on one of life's great adventures; your very own journey to *The Great Land.*

Either way, your journey will undoubtedly prove to be an experience you will always cherish.

January 1995

About This Book

The Call of the River (Dan Heiner's 3rd Book on Fly-fishing Alaska) was not written to serve as either a How-To or a Technique Book for those persons desiring fly-fishing instruction. Neither is it a book dedicated to the methods of tying Alaska fly patterns. Several other volumes of these types of books are readily available.

Instead, The Call of the River (See also "ALASKA On The Fly" 1993 and, "In Search of ALASKA's BEST FLY-FISHING" 1994) is an overview of one season of fly-fishing in Alaska with the author. Come along with Dan as he travels to and experiences several of Alaska's ultimate lodges, rivers, lakes, and streams.

The Call of the River is more of a where and a why book, rather than a 'How To' book, describing this land called Alaska and touching on many of the premier locations involved in fishing The Great Land. At the request of some Alaska lodge owners, a handful of names and whereabouts of some of Alaska's ultimate and oftentimes fragile waters (streams that are already beginning to feel too much fishing pressure) are not given.

It is hoped that the opinions, descriptions, and anecdotes given in this book will make for enjoyable reading, good trip planning, and enjoyable fly-fishing. It is also hoped that readers will find this book entertaining and informative – possibly inspiring a few, at least, to go on to experience Alaska's best fly-fishing personally. If this book might cause some readers to take up the sport of fly-fishing for the first time, any and all efforts by the author will have been worth it.

Dan Heiner

January 1995

About The Author

For over a decade now, Dan Heiner has pursued his dream of fly-fishing Alaska. In his travels he has been privileged to fish sevcral ultimate rivers, lakes, and streams, and as you will see, he has visited many Alaska Fishing Lodges.

Ever since Dan first came to Alaska, in 1983, he wanted to personally experience as much of Alaska as time would permit. To date, his journies have taken him to several regions of the state, to something approaching forty professional Alaska fishing lodges, and to something approaching fifty of Alaska's eighty-five or so premier waters.

All the while, Dan's appreciation for Alaska and its fly-fishing has continued to grow – ever since he first began exploring the state as Field Editor for *Alaska Outdoors* magazine in 1985.

Now, whenever Dan does a fishing story, be it for a fly-fishing magazine or for a book, he'll occasionally add another river or two to his list. Being a full time resident of Alaska also assists Dan in getting to know Alaska's rivers just that much better.

Ironically, when Dan first moved to Alaska, he was interested only in big game hunting, not in fly-fishing. Whenever a 'fishing' story would come along Dan would do it, "....but with a little reluctance" he recalls. Then, suddenly, the fly-fishing bug bit him and Dan became hooked on Alaska's fly-fishing. Quickly, he began to develop an appreciation for what his father had tried to teach him about the sport of fly-fishing back in the mid '60's.

Today, as a member of the G. Loomis Alaska Pro-Staff, Dan Heiner continues his quest of exploring and fly-fishing Alaska. He is an active proponent of the joys and benefits of catch-and-release fly-fishing.

Preface

Through the pages of this book, readers will come to know many real life Alaskan characters. One, Paul D. Rotkis ("Eli," as the author calls him) is a bonafide fly-fishing fanatic.

Eli virtually lives fly-fishing – from the moment he wakes up in the morning until the time he falls asleep – whenever or wherever that may be. Eli ties flies continuously, talks tackle incessantly, thinks fly-fishing totally, and fly-fishes Alaska regularly.

Over the years Eli has developed into a very experienced fly-fisher; in fact, one of the most knowledgeable and proficient the author has ever met. Eli knows Alaska's road system streams and rivers as well as anyone, it seems, and he spends a good portion of his time in summers driving to his 'secret fishing spots' when he isn't working full-time as a firefighter, and part-time at a major sporting goods dealer in Anchorage, in their fly-fishing department.

Eli is can probably best be described as one who, "...loves his wife, his country, his cats, and his fly-fishing," though not necessarily in that order. Like the author, "Eli" usually prefers fly-fishing over work. Yet, in spite of his fanatical fly-fishing obsession, Paul D. "Eli" Rotkis seems to be a happy, fairly well-adjusted individual. Best of all, Eli laughs at the author's jokes.

Another fishing partner readers will come to know in the pages of this book is, Tom Coomer, also a fly-fishing addict, a casual, giant of a man (6 feet, 5 inches, 245 lbs.) who has resided in Alaska for the past four or five years. Tom loves fly-fishing, enjoys float tubing, and has made a study of learning many of the Anchorage area's lakes. Like Eli, Tom Coomer is a better fly-fisher than the author, and his love for the sport is only exceeded by his his affection for his cocker spaniel, "Augie."

Fly-Fishing Adventure # 1

Halibut ...On A Fly?
Large, Speckled Trout

Eli's phone call came in early May offering a very interesting proposition. "Wanna come along with Tony Weaver and me for a taste of some saltwater fly-fishing?"

The previous winter had been a long one. Not a particularly cold one, but a long one, nonetheless. Consequently, I for one, was *more* than ready for spring, and *more* than a touch ready to fool around with fly rods in Alaska once again.

At the time, I'd just finished writing my second book, *In Search of* ALASKA'S BEST FLY-FISHING, which was soon to be printed, bound, and released. My advertising business in Anchorage had finally waned down to a manageable level, so I was more than ready to reaquaint myself with the art of casting a fly line.

Would I be interested in joining Eli and Tony Weaver in a couple of weeks for a little saltwater fly-fishing from a 27-foot boat motoring out of Seward?

The fly-fishing part was easy. It was the part concerning deep seas and saltwater that placed an entirely new twist on the subject.

New to me, at least.

Still, I was ready. *More* than ready.

15

Oh, I'd *heard* about fly-fishing saltwater for halibut and ling cod and the like on a fly rod – but I never dreamed of actually becoming involved in the sport.

The plan was for four of us to meet at the south parking lot of Carrs grocery store in south Anchorage at 5:00 on the morning of May 27. My good friend and fishing companion, Paul "Eli" Rotkis, would meet me at the parking lot and leave his car behind. Together, we'd drive down to Seward in my Blazer. Tony Weaver and his friend, Gordon Stewart, would meet us there, too, and we'd take two vehicles and drive down in tandem.

Naturally, I'd attempt to talk Eli into driving my Blazer while I navigated, trying to come to my senses at that early hour.

When the big day arrived, Eli was there, right on time as usual. Eli might be late for breakfast once in a while, or he might be a little tardy for work now and then, but Eli's almost never late for fly-fishing.

"You've got to have your priorities straight" he says.

Surprisingly, my watch read 4:52 a.m. when I pulled into Carrs. Since I was first to arrive, I pulled into an obvious parking stall and, leaving the engine running and the lights on, I pushed the button on the Blazer's dashboard that opens the rear tailgate.

I figured it was the least I could do to help Eli load his gear, for when Eli goes fishing, there's always plenty of gear – usually enough to outfit about a half dozen anglers.

Sure enough, two minutes later Eli pulled in alongside me. He had a big smile on his face as he always does that early in the morning. Worse, he even looked perky, like he'd been up for hours – as if he'd been tying flies or lifting weights since 3:00 a.m.

Sure enough, Eli'd completely filled one of those big, black, industrial-looking, telescoping, 6-inch diameter, 12-foot long heavy plastic rod tubes with nothing but state of the art graphite. As usual, he'd brought along enough rods and reels to outfit a National Guard battalion.

What am I getting into? I wondered as I finally worked up enough energy to greet Eli and encourage his loading efforts.

That's about when Tony and Gordon pulled up, too.

I glanced at my watch: 4:58 a.m.

And that's about when I started wondering about *my* equipment.

After all, I'd brought along but one measly fly rod: a 9-foot, 10-weight, off-brand graphite number (no names, please) a rod I'd never used before; a rod I'd recently acquired in a trade with a used sporting goods dealer across town in Spenard.

I'd needed another fly rod like I needed another Dachshund in the backyard, but the deal *was* a good one – besides, I'd never actually *owned* a 10-weight fly rod before.

That rod wasn't something I'd been out looking for, mind you. I'd have probably opted for a G. Loomis IMX or one of the super-light GLX models if I'd been in the market for a serious 10-weight, but the deal was a good one and the rod so adequate (no, better than adequate) that I simply had to act then or forever live with the guilt. Cost vs. benefits considered, I decided to grab the rod and worry about what I'd tell the boys at Loomis later.

Along with the 10-weight, I'd brought along my heaviest reel (at the time) an 8/9 direct drive salmon reel (likewise, no names, please) a combination that was a fairly decent salmon outfit but probably wasn't the perfect reel for going after halibut on a fly. However, it *was* the stoutest reel I owned at the time. Like I've said, it's a fine reel, but I wasn't sure it was the right reel to use for going after fish the size of barn doors.

On that reel I had my fastest-sinking fly line, a Teeny T-400, complete with its attractive, yellow running line section and its integral, dark brown, 24-foot fast sinking sinktip section. That line is a dandy for deep water salmon and steelhead, but a poor excuse for a saltwater line – but it *was* the best I had, so...

Eli awakened me when we finally pulled in to Seward, praising me for the fine job of navigating I'd done. I don't actually remember much of the drive although I'm sure it was pretty and it probably took a couple of hours. It usually does.

I glanced at my watch: 6:57 a.m.

I don't exactly remember climbing out of the Blazer and walking over to upper boat dock, but I must have, for I soon found myself standing over there, holding my new 10-weight fly rod in one hand and summoning Eli with the other.

By that time, both Tony and Gordon had already boarded the 27-foot aluminum boat we'd be going out on. Finally, after a bit more coaxing, Eli managed to lug all of his gear down to the dock.

Jimmy Seas, of *The Charter Connection* in Seward, was to be our captain and guide that day. His boat looked to be a dandy, and best of all I spied a comfortable mattress where I could flop out for another hour or so while I continued coming to my senses.

It didn't take long for Jimmy Seas to prove to be a master seaman. Best of all, he is the sort of individual who's fun to be

around. Like many Alaskans, Jimmy's an extremely colorful
character – along with being an outstanding guide who proved to
have an excellent knowledge of the area. Jimmy had an excellent
assistant with him on his custom, new, aluminum inboard boat,
but, unfortunately, I've forgotten that fellow's name.

After motoring out of Seward Harbor, our first quest,
naturally, was to head for where the halibut would be found.
During the voyage, Jimmy Seas reminded us that we should not be
particular in any future communications about *where* this
adventure might take us.

"Heck, that's easy," I assured him. "The older I get the easier
it is for me to forget things – I do it all the time." Especially like
where we were in the heck we were out there on those big, blue,
wide-open seas that cool morning in May, anyway. To be honest,
I don't believe I could have pointed to where Seward was in
relation to wherever it was we were, anyway. Besides, I still
wasn't awake yet.

I glanced at my watch: 7:46 a.m.

Eventually we arrived at Jimmy Seas' secret hole, wherever it
is. All I knew was, there was water all around us and people
around me who were beginning to act excited and assemble their
fly rods – people beginning to act real serious all of a sudden.

I glanced at my watch: 7:57 a.m.

Somehow I summoned the courage to assemble my new, used
fly rod and salmon reel and I step out on the casting deck with the
big boys.

Where ever it was we were, Jimmy Seas' secret halibut hole
soon turned out to be the Mother of all Saltwater Fishin' Holes

because things started happenin,' and people started shoutin,' and fish started bitin' – *fast*.

Considering the size of the fish we were going after, I felt more than a little silly about getting out there on the deck of Jimmy Seas' boat, stringin-up my little, dime-store 10-weight fly rod. Actually, I felt more than a little like a kid out there on the salt with his 'new' used toy.

Just out doin' a days' fishin' with the big boys, I was.

While the rest of the guys were busy rigging up their fairly expensive, very business-like, 12-weight fly rod systems, I found myself counting seagulls and searching my pockets for previously used gum wrappers and other incidentals. Not that my fly rod was *that* bad, mind you – even if the thing *did* only have about six snake guides all together – but somehow, all of a sudden, just having a 10-weight out there felt pretty light and pretty silly.

Fly-fishing for *halibut?* With a 10-weight?

Eli, on the other hand, took occasion and special measure to show off his brand spanking new, lovely, extra-shiny, jewel-like, nicely finished, state of the art, anti-reverse Billy Pate Tarpon fly reel. For those not familiar with that particular model, *cavernous* probably best describes it – with a drag that *could* stop a train.

Eli and Tony had previously experienced this saltwater fly-fishing stuff in the past, but Gordon, thank heaven, was as new to the salt as I was.

In fact, Tony, Eli, and Gordon were *all* well equipped for fly-fishing for halibut, come to think of it. For one thing, Tony *sells* fly-fishing equipment (need any new stuff?) so, naturally, both Tony and Gordon had all the heavy fly rods and reels a fellow could ask for. Eli, on the other hand, *works* part-time in a fly-fishing department at a fine sporting goods store. Consequently, over the seasons he's assembled a fairly impressive collection of toys.

"Tools," Eli describes 'em. "Necessary tools."

What it came down to basically, was, *they* were ready for halibut and ling cod – *they* were also ready for king salmon, for large, fresh chums, for silvers (if any should happen along), heck, they were ready for flounder for that matter. In fact, Tony Weaver was almost ready for the 10-foot salmon shark that suddenly swam alongside the boat and gobbled his fly when he lowered it – but that's a story best saved for another chapter.

10-foot Salmon Sharks? Where the heck are we, Eli?

I glanced at my watch: 8:43 a.m.

The way their 850-grain shooting heads were casting and sinking –and quickly getting down– Eli and Tony proved to be light years ahead of me when it came to saltwater tackle, understanding, and techniques. But then, this was nothing new. Eli has always been light years ahead of me in most types of fly-fishing endeavors we've undertaken. Then again, he should be: Eli fly-fishes more than any other living human being I've ever encountered. And Tony? Tony *sells* the stuff.

"Hey, Eli! Mind if I borrow one of your size 6/0, white halibut zonkers?"

Finally, after what seemed like forever, my Teeny T-400 sinktip line began the turn from horizontal to vertical as it slowly began to sink out there in that big, deep-blue Alaska sea. A very gentle, lazy sinking motion it was, however – but I wasn't complaining; this fly-fishing for halibut was fast becoming fun stuff, even if it did seem a bit weird and more than slightly different than casting size-12 Stimulators on a 4-weight.

Just for a minute, there, I felt a little like a Lefty Kreh or possibly a Trey Combs or one of those other big name fly-fishers – *just out doin' a days' work* – but then I glanced down at my fly rod again and realized I'd be lucky just to hook a fish, let alone actually *land* one of them monsters.

Finally, after what seemed like an hour – but was really only seven or eight minutes – my fly line *did* assume a vertical position. To help my fly reach bottom, I'd stripped off several additional yards of 30-pound micron backing from the spool.

What *was* down there possibly looking over my 6/0 white zonker? I wondered.

About the time I felt my fly touch bottom, I figured I was something like 130 to 140 feet down (thank goodness Eli had remembered to bring the flies). Then, attempting to mimic what the others were doing, I began jigging my fly up and down, up and down, ever so slightly.

Jigging. *Yeah*, that's what they call this. "I believe they call this type of fishing jigging, don't they, Eli?"

This isn't fly-fishing, I thought to myself.

Suddenly, almost before I knew it, something very big and very austere and very much alive grabbed my fly, bending my newly acquired, used, No-name fly rod over almost double. Suddenly, my new 10-weight fly rod felt more like a mere 3-weight in my hands. I looked over at Eli, who was now laughing and had a smirky glint in his eye.

"Told you you'd like it!" he said.

At first I thought maybe I'd hooked a snag, but the boat wasn't idling, so whatever it was, *it was alive*, and whatever it was was soon began peeling off backing *like* a freight train.

Suddenly my "adequate" salmon reel seemed more like a replica out of a Kellogg's box than it did a bonafide fishing reel. Whatever it was that had grabbed my fly was pulling hard – I mean *really* pulling. All of a sudden, line was peeling-off my spool like I'd latched onto a semitruck. Quickly, I double-checked my drag setting.

Sure enough, *Full*.

"Holy Sailfish, Eli," I hollered. "What have you got me into this time? Isn't this reel supposed to stop trains?"

Looking back, now, I believe I'd hooked a halibut. But I'll never really know for certain, because that monster whateveritwas never did stop, even for a second, and all of a sudden the hook pulled free. All I know is that it *felt* like I'd hooked into a 900-pounder. More than likely, it was only something like a very decent, 40-pound halibut, but, like I say, I guess I'll never really know – for certain.

It *felt* like a freight train.

I looked over at Tony who, by this time had hooked a 'whateveritwas,' too. He were also busy, pumping, reeling, pumping, reeling...laughing heartily, but more than anything reeling in for all his worth.

23

When I cranked in the remainder of my loose line, all I had to show for my efforts was a small chunk of slimy, white, slightly scaly tissue. So I hadn't been imagining. For all I knew whateveritwas I'd hooked very well might have been a corner of the world's record lingcod's mouth, even though chances were that it was only a very average sized halibut.

"They call this fly-fishing, Eli?"

I glanced at my watch: 10:28 a.m.

(A couple of weeks after our trip, someone informed me that Mike Hood had, in fact, *caught* the world's record lingcod on a fly: *28 pounds*, not to mention the world's record halibut he also landed about the same time: *90 pounds*).

Record halibut – and lingcod – *On a fly!*

Pretty soon, Eli hollered. His rod was bent, too. Apparently he'd hooked into a dandy of a whateveritis, also.

I watched him play it for a while, methodically working the rod up and down, up and down, reeling just at the right instant, bringing that big whatever it was to bay within only twelve or fifteen minutes. It turned out to be a fine, respectable halibut, a 47-pounder to be exact, a fish that was quickly netted by Captain Jimmy Seas, who was by this time whooping and hollering, sounding just like Eli, encouraging Eli's effort with full bravado.

Way to go, *Eli!*

Come to think of it, Eli's halibut might have *been* a world record – for a few days, at least – although Eli never did brag much about its size in front of the others. It was only after the trip that Eli raved about the size of that fish and the power that fish had dished out. I wouldn't say he was boasting, but he did keep talking about it, and talking about it, and...

After all, how many people in the first place are in the habit of venturing out, fly-fishing for halibut? All I knew was that Eli had just done a fine job of angling - along with a nice job of filling my freezer for the coming winter.

Forty-seven pounds of nice fly-fishing, Eli!

I quickly reached for my pocket camera and snapped-off a couple of pictures of the event, forever capturing Eli, his eyes twinkling, holding that prized flatfish of his. That twinkle told me Eli had had fun fishing – always a nice thing to accomplish along the way, world's record or no.

Tony Weaver nearly landed a very large flatfish on a flyrod this day (he did a couple of weeks later) but, alas, like mine, at the very last moment, somehow that big whatever it was from the depths managed to slip the hook. As always, Tony remained a good sport about it.

"*Drats!*" Another lost fish for the memory book.

Sensing the opportunity for filling the freezer like Eli had, Gordon and I soon stooped to picking up stout saltwater rods, each of us promptly hooking halibut. As I recall, it didn't take Gordon very long. I was just wishing something would grab my bait when . . .*wham!*

Fishing for halibut in 350 or 400 feet of water amidst rolling waves usually isn't one of my favorite angling activities. On the other hand, this "shallow" water, clear, calm-day kind of halibut fishing was different. There we were, fishing in only about 130 feet of water, with a flatfish 'taking' on nearly every drop – and it could be done using either a fly rod *or* a bait rod, depending on the quality of your line and/or reel and the mood you were in at the time.

I would have boated one on a fly rod, had I the right tackle that day. *Honest.*

Still, I found myself enjoying this new-to-me, lighter rod and reel method of fly-fishing for halibut. Usually, I absolutely detest lugging one of those heavy lead ball weights up and down all day when fishing using conventional methods. For a minute there I even considered tying on a size-4 Egg Sucking Leech and possibly catching a 5-pound flatfish, suddenly becoming the world's record holder using the world's smallest fly. But that's about when I got to thinking straight again.

Actually, Tony didn't catch that huge, ugly lingcod that Jimmy Seas helped him land; that repulsive creature from the depths had hooked its jaws around a small, juicy flatfish Tony had hooked –*yes*, a double wammy– and, yes, Jimmy Seas managed to net both travelers from the deep and hoist the whole works up into the boat. *Amazing*, just like Tony's smile. One of the most amazing fishing feats I've ever witnessed.

Frankly, the idea of obtaining some halibut for the freezer did make *some* sense. I'm generally a strict, catch and release sort, myself, especially when it comes to rainbow trout. But, after all, fresh flatfish does make for delicious dining, and I wasn't about to look a gift horse in the mouth.

Fairly soon the hold of Jimmy Seas' boat was filled with our legal limit of fresh, tantalizing halibut. I forget what the actual limit per man was, but Jimmy Seas kept watching, always counting, ever keeping track of the numbers of fish we landed. When we reached the magic number, Jimmy Seas firmly and promptly told us, *"That's all, folks!"*

I reached for my trusty camera and quickly fired off a couple photos of 25 and 30-pound, very delicious, but very average sized Alaska halibut.

With the speckled flatfish now out of the way it was time for lunch. Tasty soft drinks and sandwiches, along with some good laughs out on those high seas, breathing that crisp, clean air. Occassionally a salmon (what kind?) would jump, apparently 'jus lookin' around, tryin' to recapture its direction.

Where the heck IS Resurrection Bay from here anyway, Sally?

I had to admit it'd been an amazing morning and it was humorous for each of us to recall the wild and furious action we'd each experienced. As a sort of tribute, the four of us dubbed the place "Jimmy's Gloryhole," whereever it is, and promptly made a pact that we'd never divulge its whereabouts to anyone.

Here's to Jimmy Seas' Gloryhole – wherever it was.

It was fun to watch Gordon out there on the first fishing expedition of his life. Gordon really got into it, catching fish like crazy – just like Eli and Tony Weaver had done. Gordon's the very strong, well-proportioned, eat-the-right-diet, weight-lifter, body-builder type. In fact, I heard later that Gordon is a physical fitness trainer for Olympic Downhill Skiing Champion Tommy Moe. Whenever Gordon hooked a fish, which turned out to be frequently, he'd have the advantage in the strength department. But by the way he was laughing, it didn't take a physics professor to ascertain that he was having the time of his life.

Naturally, Eli was pleased with having landed such a fine halibut, for it added to his list another specie he'd taken on the fly.

Eli's the kind of guy that gets out there and just does it. Like I've mentioned, Paul "Eli" Rotkis is one of the most experienced, most versatile flyrodders I've ever met. Whereas most of us stick to one form of fishing, say, dry flies and rainbows, or drifting 'coho' flies for 'reds,', Eli is always out there, attempting this new specie or that new technique – all with a fly. Eli fishes ALL species of Alaska's sport fish, be it fresh water or saltwater, from mid-May to late October, from 4:00 a.m. to midnight. The killer part is, Eli's wife even *supports* his obsession.

After lunch it was time to attempt an entirely different type of saltwater fly-fishing.

Different to me, at least.

"You'll really like it!" Eli shouted over the spray of the engine, as Jimmy Seas goosed the husky Volvo inboard and began motoring to a spot over by the cliffs where he promised us we'd hook into more than our share of black sea bass.

Eli and Tony had both experienced this type of fishing before, too, so I just sat back and watched closely as they rigged their long, 7-weight fly rods.

I noticed they both used floating lines. Since it was the only rod I had with me, naturally I found myself reaching for 'ol reliable, my 9-foot, 10-weight, the 'ol, No-Name again. Although I *did* have a floater with me on another spool, I didn't switch lines – not just yet, anyway. I'd wait and observe closely for a minute or two just to see what this black bass fly-fishing stuff was all about.

When we got to Jimmy's secret spot, Eli made a surface presentation using a size 4 White Zonker (as usual), fishing it much like a schoolboy drags a worm across the top for the first time. Suddenly, an ugly black snout rocketed up from the depths and attacked the zonker, a hookup that came in what seemed like only six or seven seconds. Suddenly a dark, spiny, bug-eyed, charcoal black sea bass had appeared out of nowwhere and engulfed Eli's wet fly, half swallowing it, hooking itself firmly in the process.

Next thing I knew, Eli and Tony were laughing almost uncontrollably. It *was* kinda funny, come to think of it, so Gordon and I couldn't help but begin laughing too. One minute there was nothing but ocean surface to see and the next a score of bug-eyed bass would suddenly appear up out of the depths like they'd materialized out of nowhere. The amazing thing was, there were what seemed to be endless numbers of them that would rise to almost any of our presentations.

Disturbing the water didn't seem to spook 'em. The more commotion we created the more it only seemed to excite them.

"This isn't a fishin' hole, *it's an aquarium!*" I exclaimed to the others.

"Yeah! The Aquarium," Tony replied, "That's what we'll have to call this place!"

"*Yeah*, The Aquarium!" Eli agreed.

Sensing the action, Gordon promptly cast out what looked to be a size 3/4oz. Pixie over in the same general direction. Almost immediately, yet another black bass appeared and quickly grabbed Gordon's offering.

It's funny how a new specie can affect you at times. Here, I'd never even seen a *black* sea bass before (hardly even knew they existed) and yet, there they were, coming up to the surface in numbers, attacking our flies – and whatever else we threw at them – like the rainbows of my wildest dreams, like they hadn't had a decent meal in months. I quickly found myself developing a genuine fondness for this aggressive, homely, yet tasty saltwater specie.

"They're almost as delicious as halibut" Jimmy Seas kept telling us, reinforcing the rationale of keeping a few for the freezer. "You're each allowed to keep up to (five?) bass apiece, they're great eating!" he added.

It was about then that Eli produced his infamous, "Noodle Rod," a very long, super flimsy creation he'd assembled utilizing graphite bait casting blanks. It's a ridiculously long rod, about a 13-footer, a fly-rod that flops well over to one side when extended.

"*It's an absolutely perfect opportunity for the Noodle!*" Eli proclaimed with a grin. Disbelieving what I was seeing, I took another long look at the strange, extra-long, ultra thin rod Eli held.

"*You actually use that thing?*" I asked.

I'd go on to tell you more about that 10-foot salmon shark Tony Weaver hooked on a fly, and the huge, twin humpback whales that swam directly beneath our 27-foot aluminum boat – but no one would probably believe me, anyway. Just like I could hardly believe the action we'd experienced out there that day – out there on the deep, blue salty seas with Captain Jimmy Seas, fishing with The Charter Connection. Eventually we motored our way from where ever it was we were out on that ocean back to Seward Boat Harbor.

Later that night, after cleaning fish for a couple of hours and after vigorously thanking and tipping Jimmy Seas and his assistant, we finally left Seward for the drive back to Anchorage. Back to *civilization.*

I glanced at my watch: 9:28 p.m.

Eli volunteered to drive, so I volunteered to navigate. I had to admit; it *had* been quite a day – a day of fly-fishing action unlike any I'd ever experienced before.

Several vivid impressions of that day are imbedded in my memory: Eli standing out on that deck, muscling in what was possibly the world's record halibut *ever* taken on a fly rod 'til that time. . . Tony, with that chunky, 10-foot salmon shark suddenly on his hook. . . those two curious behemoths, those giant humpbacks, gliding silently under our boat. . .the power of that *what ever it was* I'd hooked right off the bat.

Back in Anchorage we made a quick stop at Safeway to pick up some freezer bags. Three hours later we finally finished dividing the halibut and rockfish for the freezer. I waived Eli godspeed, thanking him for the chance to learn about a new type of fly-fishing.

I glanced at my watch: 2:49 a.m.

I'd be hedging to say that I didn't find myself wandering over to Mountain View Sports that next day. Spying what I quickly recognized as being a "steal," I prompty latched onto a larger, much more expensive reel, a reel having a much stouter drag than the reel I'd used on my maiden saltwater fly-fishing voyage. Of course, along with that new, expensive reel I *had* to have an extra fast sinking, 850-grain shooting taper and 350 yards of 30 lb. micron backing to go with it. Never mind their costs.

Necessary tools.

I don't know what got into me; maybe I was thinking I might just return and try for halibut again one of these days.

But as time went on I found myself *thinking* about that trip that day in late May when the four of us crazy anglers had had the time of our lives fly-fishing at unknown places named The Gloryhole and The Aquarium, out there *somewhere* on a deep, blue, seemingly-endless ocean, out where seagulls and arctic terns frolicked in the breezes and where humpback and killer whales playfully cruised about the boat.

On a good day those are indeed happy places, places out there somewhere on the salt where fly-fishers can shout and laugh at one another and have the time of their lives. But they're Jimmy Seas' secret places – places I couldn't begin to remember where they are today if I had to.

Fly-Fishing Adventure #2
LAKE I LI-AM-NA
Iliamna Lake Resort

The preceding winter hadn't been such a cold one, really, even though at times it *had* seemed like the season that wouldn't end.

Some winters in Alaska are like that. Then, just about the time a fly-fisher decides spring is permanently on hold, presto – the sun breaks through. By that time, dreams of rainbow trout dancing at the surface are often all that exist between a fly-fisher and an advanced case of cabin fever to sustain him through those final six weeks.

Of course, Alaska has seven distinct seasons, really: (1) a two month, fairly dark period called, early winter; (2) a two month, very dark period called, mid winter; (3) a two month, fairly dark period called, late winter; (4) a particularly cold, 10-day period Alaskans refer to as Fur Rendezvous, always a frigid 10-day period when people flock to downtown Anchorage and real Alaskans walk around wearing fox pelts draped over their heads and shoulders; (5) a one month thawing spell Alaskans refer to as, "Winter Break-Up," a period when Alaska becomes the undisputed windshield washer fluid capitol of the world and a drive around the block oftentimes seems more like a McKinley excursion; (6) summer, a *glorious*, three and a half month period following 'Final Break Up' when the sun tends to hang in the sky for nearly twenty-four hours a day and some days actually *do* get to 80 degrees, where once in a while a rainbow trout or two may be caught, and, finally; (7) VET (Volcano Eruption Time), usually a three week transition period occurring between summer and early winter (approximately every other year) when fly-fishers suddenly learn that all flights to Iliamna and Katmai have been cancelled and it's difficult to determine whether the stuff falling from the sky is ash or snow. Usually, VET lasts only until about October 16, when *more* white stuff falls from the sky and finally, *it is* snowing. Then, all of a sudden it's winter once again in Alaska.

Don't get me wrong. It's not that flyfishers mind winters in Alaska so much – anticipation has long been a favorite punishment of many an Alaskan – it's just that visions of leaping rainbow trout are frequently all there are to assist flyfishing Alaskans to retain even a touch of sanity, a sort of a neutral zone between bonafide insanity and simple, everyday, common cabin fever.

Then finally, April comes, and with it, The Great Alaska Sportsman's Show, signaling the coming end of winter and possibly the chance to actually fly-fish once again and thus renew one's sense of selfworth.

It was at the last Sportsman's Show that my fly-fishing season started. I'd bumped into Jimmy Winchester and Masao Kikuchi, co–hosts at *Iliamna Lake Resort*. Jimmy and Masao were at their booth across the isle from the guy who sells plastic ice scrapers and 'easy to use' whatchmacallits for tying fishing knots. *"Purchase a knot widget and we'll throw in a free ice scraper!"*

Would I be interested in joining Jimmy and Masao over at Iliamna Lake Resort for three or four days of fly-fishing?

Hmmm. Let me think about that for a while.

Ten minutes later, back at the G. Loomis booth, Tony Weaver and Mike Hood mentioned something about filming a fly-fishing video for Prime Sports Northwest. "Possibly something over Iliamna way" – something to do with dry flies and rainbow trout.

Would I care to help them select a lodgethat would assist them in their efforts?

Hmmm. Let me think about that for a while.

I was just beginning to think I'd suddenly received more than my annual allotment of good fortune when Les Jacober and Tony Sarp, of *Tony Sarp's* KATMAI LODGE, on the famed Alagnak River, informed me of an opening in mid-June, smack dab during the middle of the caddis hatch.

"Bring your 3-weight" Les said with a grin.

It's strange how opportunities often *do* come in threes, but a couple of days later, Bernie Ortman disproved that theory when he called from Whitehorse, informing me that there was room enough for two fly-fishers in late June at his fabulous Wood River Lodge. Would I like to stop out?

A tear of joy nearly came to my eye as I looked up heavenward and offered a secret (and very sincere) thank you. Maybe there is life after advertising, afterall I decided. Then it occurred to me, 'I'll bet Eli might just like it over in the Tikchiks.'

Naturally, I'd wanted to tell my wife all about the good news, but somehow I just couldn't find words for my upcoming adventures just then. Besides, some things are better left unsaid until all the pieces are in place – which they weren't.

Yet.

For one thing, I'd have to carefully arrange things back at the office to keep my advertising clients happy – or just keep clients, period. Still, I had to admit: two lodges *were* right there at Lake Iliamna, just across the lake from each other. The third, KATMAI LODGE, could be reached via bushplane within only another hour's flight. The fourth, Wood River Lodge, could be reached in only another hour and a half's flying time – fly-fishing gods permitting, that is.

Still, it wasn't until about two months later (when I found myself packing, readying for the drive to the airport) that I remembered I'd forgotten to tell my wife what it was I was doing. Oh, she knew I was going fishing, all right – so what else was there? The part about when I'd be coming home again was the only part that hadn't come up.

Yet.

Fifty-five minutes by commercial airliner and twelve minutes by van ride later I arrived at the doorstep of beautiful Iliamna Lake Resort, an ultimate, 28-unit condo /lodge facility that somehow looks more like something that should be named, Palm Desert Golf Resort and Fishing Club, but, it's a lodge, all right.

The minute I arrived I recognized ILR's chief pilot, Chris Smith, whom I'd met a couple of years earlier while fishing out

Iliamna way with John Gierach. Chris had worked as a pilot for a competing lodge at the time.

Chris is the kind of Alaska pilot who really loves to fly. Actually, he's the kind of pilot who literally lives to fly. From having watched him closely, I rank him among the best bush pilots I've ever flown with.

Over the years Chris has developed a deep love and affinity for all types of flying machines, although he has developed a particular affection for de Havilland's 9-cylinder, radial-engined, "Beaver" model. (Funny, ILR just happened to have a newly rebuilt, pretty, blue and white Kenmore-modified and refurbished deHavilland Beaver.)

For those who may not know, de Havilland Beavers are widely regarded as being Alaska's most dependable workhorses. They're easily Alaska's most coveted bushplanes.

Produced from 1947 to 1967, Beavers are today as popular in Alaska as they are in Canada. Only 1,631 beavers were ever produced, and the U.S. military purchased something like 981 of them. Beavers are powered by a single Pratt and Whitney, 9-cylinder, radial engine which develops 450 horsepower.

It goes without saying that Beavers will handle a sizeable payload – easily accomodating five passengers *and* their belongings – which, coupled with their ability to take-off in short distances, makes Beavers highly revered by Alaska's fishing lodges. "If a Beaver will float, it will fly" is a common description of these large, dependable bushplanes. Newer, single-engine airplanes – such as the Cessna 180, 182, 185 and 206 series – all fly faster than a Beaver will, but none of them even comes close to what a

Beaver can carry. Piper's Super Cub, the supreme bush plane of them all when it comes to sheer maneuverability and performance, is simply too small for most lodge requirements.

One evening after dinner Chris and I spent nearly four hours reflecting about the various lakes and rivers found in that part of Alaska and the airplanes best suited to reach them. It was fascinating comparing notes, as both of us had come to know many of the same characters in our travels.

The next day, June 8, would be the opening day of fishing season in that area. Time to get out the ol' rod and reel and limber up the ol' casting arm. From what the boys at Alaska Fish & Game had said, by June 8 the rainbows have finally finished their spawning chores. Here it was, June 7. The opening of fishing was nearly upon us. Somehow I just *happened* to find myself in Iliamna, Alaska.

Chris was all smiles that next morning as he strolled down the dirt road from the lodge. Rounding Slopbucket Lake, he headed directly for the Beaver. In one hand he carried his flight log, and in the other his flight jacket. He was a pilot on a mssion who, like the rest of us, had waited many long months for another fishing season to begin.

A half hour later, Chris was still smiling like a kid who'd just gotten glimpse of his first Schwinn as he sat there in the pilot's seat, engine idling, just sitting there, listening to the purr of that big, dependable, Pratt and Whitney radial.

Presently, four of us fly-fishers stumbled down and piled in the side door, securing our seats behind Chris. Jimmy Winchester, who was just shy of receiving his own private pilot's license at the time, hopped in the right seat, up front alongside Chris. That Beaver is a beauty; as I buckled my seat belt I noticed the new, grey, leather seats and headliner that'd only recently been installed.

Our first stop would be the confluence of where a small creek flows into Iliamna, less than a ten minute ride and only a few short miles along the shoreline from where the mighty Newhalen River enters into the mother lake.

As we approached and circled the creek somebody shouted, "I see fish!" Naturally, everybody stared into the riffles. Cutting the power and lowering the flaps, Chris proceeded to gently set the Beaver down on the waves of Iliamna. Then, powering the airplane around, facing away from the beach, Chris cut the engine as we drifted back into shore. That Beaver bobbed like a cork on those 2-foot Iliamna swells.

For me, it's always exciting stuff, this flying out, adventuring-off to the wilds of Alaska - knowing that as far as rainbow trout and grayling and char fly-fishing goes, it simply doesn't get any better than what The Last Frontier has to offer. I have to admit, there are few places on earth I'd rather be on the opening day of fishing season than in Alaska's Iliamna, Katmai, or Bristol Bay regions. Just being out there, somewhere in *the rainbow zone,* exploring one or two of those famous creeks I'd spent all winter dreaming about was enough for me – fish or no fish. It's the very stuff my dreams are made of.

Sculpins in various shades of pale and dark could be seen scurrying in the tundra pools we crossed, as the four of us fly-fishers scrambled a couple of hundred yards over the tundra to that swolen creek.

Judging by the tracks they'd left behind, a moose and her calf had only recently vacated the area. Other tracks told us that a couple of days earlier a small bear had meandered around down by that creek. It'd been a brownie, all right, but since no salmon were in the stream this early in the season, I figured there was little chance the bear had discovered a meal.

Naturally, our immediate objective was to reconnoiter the stream conditions as quickly as possible. We wanted to ascertain whether its waters contained anything interesting, such as anything at all that resembled 'leopards,' - a term Alaska's fly-fishing guides use in describing rainbow trout. As all fly-fishers know, rainbows have a way of shifting haunts at the drop of a hat, so what might have been dynamite fishing yesterday doesn't always mean it will be good today or again tomorrow. Even in Alaska.

Scottie Turo (one of the lodge's young guides, out on his very first expedition) and I ventured upstream a ways - while lodge manager Jim Winchester and another young guide, Kurt Armacost, elected to probe the mysteries of the riffles nearer the lake.

Scottie and I flailed the water for a few minutes – it felt really good to cast a fly line once again – but neither of us even so much as saw a fish.

Then Kurt, who'd wandered down near the mouth, whooped at the top of his lungs. Turning, we could see he'd hooked into what looked to be a nice, four or five- pound rainbow that had struck at the black leech pattern he'd been using.

There's...one...two...three.. nice jumps.

Good for Kurt, that lucky so and so, I thought, as I tried to handle his success rationally, avoiding looking over at Scottie.

But, despite Kurt's rainbow, it wasn't long before the rest of us learned that for the most part, this particular creek just wasn't ready to be fished yet. It was still a bit too early in the season. Something just wasn't right; the water seemed simply too sterile and too cold, and straining as hard as we could, none of the rest of us could glimpse a fish to save our lives.

But none of us were disappointed. Especially Kurt. After all, the opening of fishing season in Alaska was still but a couple hours old. On the contrary, we'd all enjoyed just getting out, stretching our legs and exploring a little.

Kinda makes a guy feel like a kid again.

Back at the floatplane it was time to make another decision. Where to go from here? We still had all the time in the world to fly, explore – and fly-fish.

Jimmy and Chris both seemed to like my suggestion that we fly over to the south side of Iliamna where we could power up, over the abandoned radar site and then down, towards Kukaklek (one of the two major lakes that form the headwaters of the famed Alagnak, or Branch River).

By this time the winds had begun fairly howling (it can blow at times at Iliamna), so Chris began the second leg of our journey with a smirk on his face that told me he welcomed this challenge. By slipping the Beaver sideways through a strong, quartering tailwind, I noticed we'd begun to move along – very quickly, indeed.

Glancing at Chris, I noticed his calm, familiar smile that assured me he was a bush pilot totally in his element. Chris is one of those rare individuals who'd rather sit out in and airplane and *watch* people fish than actually wet his waders and hold a fishing rod. Chris Smith is totally infatuated with airplanes, and no matter what the elements might be, Chris usually wears a smile whenever he's sitting in the pilot's seat. Over the years he's logged thousands of hours flying in several of Alaska's remote "bush" areas.

Like I said, the ground was moving along very quickly indeed. Standard de Havilland Beavers are only designed to fly at around 95 m.p.h. –or thereabouts– but *this* particular tailwind had us traveling at nearly 120 m.p.h. - or maybe even a bit faster. Almost before we knew it, we'd crossed the 30-mile width of Iliamna, and now, vast miles of rolling, open tundra were streaking by below.

Here and there we'd spot small, ragged-looking bands of caribou - each animal looking very pale and shaggy, and more than a bit tattered after a surviving another long Alaska winter.

From my window behind Chris I could see we were fast approaching Kukaklek, a large lake that is a prime Alaska fishery. Then, sure enough, over to the left flowed the stream that John Gierach, DeWitt Daggett III and I had fly-fished a couple of summers earlier while fishing with Ted Gerken's Iliaska Lodge. I hadn't forgotten two of those rainbows I'd hooked in that creek. They'd both grabbed a leech pattern I'd bounced along the bottom (on a Teeny T-200 sink-tip) so vigorously that they'd nearly torn the rod from my hands.

Ah, Alaska fly-fishing memories.

I also remembered that just a little farther around the lake is beautiful Battle Creek - a stream that mysteriously contains too high a Ph level to sustain a constant rainbow trout population. Ironically, Battle is superb grayling water, and it's utterly beautiful, but one of the reasons it became famous over the years was probably because of the writings of internationally famous fly-fisher Lee Wulff.

Flying over Kukaklek Lake, we could see that the wind was stirring the waves below far too much to attempt a landing. There would be no taxiing or tie-down at Blueberry Creek this day. Worse, to our right, at the outlet of the lake, a minimum of four floatplanes could be seen - each with a belly-load of clients out flailing the water. Straining to see, I could barely make out the tiny dots that were the sillhouttes of individual fly-fishers adorning the shallows.

There was no decision for us, really, but to continue on. We decided unanimously to press on to Kukaklek's twin, Nonvianuk Lake. We'd check out conditions over that way.

Since Nonvianuk is only a few minutes farther south by air, this presented no big obstacle. Better yet, Nonvianuk's fly-fishing is every bit as premier as Kukaklek's. And, since some of the best char fishing in Alaska exists in this region, no one had any objections whatsoever about taking a little time and searching for a likely-looking char spot.

"Would we be interested in a little fly-fishing for arctic char instead of going for rainbows?" Jimmy queried, looking back over his shoulder. He didn't have to wait long for our answer; I'm sure our smiles said it all.

At Nonvianuk we kept flying. In those winds we sort of had to. Another canyon or two over we came to a couple of pretty lakes and a low, nearly motionless but very ominous-looking storm cloud. I glanced at Chris at the stick, who seemed totally unphased by the presence of the cloud.

A couple of minutes later we spotted a small cove that Chris said would provide a safe landing and give us some protection from the wind. "I think it might just provide us with some good fishing, too" Jimmy said with a big grin.

We circled the area carefully, keeping our eyes on the trees for any sign of wind shift. After a couple of circles, and after estimating the speed and direction of the wind, Chris finally cut the throttle, lowered the flaps, and finessed the Beaver down to his target, veering brilliantly at the last moment over some treetops before quickly regaining position and finally touching down on the lake's outlet. From there we taxied into a protected bay.

"You keep practicing your flying and one of these days you're bound to get the hang of it," I teased Chris over his shoulder.

"Yeah! Nice flying, Chris!" Scottie said.

"I'll second that!" Jimmy joined in. Kurt, who's the quiet type, just smiled.

A couple of minutes later, when the floats touched the beach we all jumped out and secured the airplane. Then we began rigging our rods. Something was telling us we'd just found ourselves a very nice little fishing spot.

Just there, a small, clear channel meanders lazily from the lake. At the surface we could see where a sizeable hatch of tiny black flies appeared to be gaining the attentions of more than a fair number of fish – that we soon began to notice.

"Gotta be rainbows" someone said.

Instinctively, I found myself reaching for a size-14 Griffith's gnat, the smallest Griffith's I had with me at the time.

I smeared a slight amount of fly floatant on both my fly and the leader, and began casting. Jim and Scottie followed suit, casting from where they stood over on the opposite bank. When I hollered over, "what flys are you guys using?" they informed me that, they, too, had opted for small, dark, gnat patterns.

Four of us fished for ten minutes with fish feeding at the surface all around us. Amazingly, however, not one of us experienced a strike.

"How strange," Jimmy said shaking his head.

"Yeah, what's the deal?" I queried.

Puzzled, I bummed a smaller gnat from Scottie and continued casting.

Still nothing.

Five minutes later, Jimmy hooked a fish.

"*Yes !*" Jimmy shouted. "It's a b o u t time!"

From the bend in Jimmy's rod, his fish looked to be about a five pounder. But when it didn't break the surface and go for the moon it started to dawn on me that we'd been fishing not for rainbows, but for char, all along.

What we'd been witnessing, we surmised, was a school of char feeding on midges very near the surface - possibly emergers – a feeding sight I'd never before seen in my travels in Alaska. From what I'd experienced and heard from others, it's seldom that char and Dollies feed at the surface — yet *this* school apparently had been doing just that.

But why those char wouldn't take any of our dry fly offerings remained a mystery until I asked Jimmy what fly did you use to catch that char.

After a minute or so Jimmy looked up and smiled. "I tied on a smolt pattern!" he admitted.

"A SMOLT?"

Thirty seven seconds and one cast later my rod was also bent — just like Jimmy's — to a robust, four and a half or five-pound char. My pet, 9 1/2-foot 6-weight G. Loomis fly rod (a rod that proved to be the perfect tool for that situation) was nearly doubled from the fight of that gold and silver speckled beauty.

Obviously the smolt pattern Jimmy Winchester showed me how to tie the evening before had been just what those char had wanted. For lack of a better name, and as a triubute to Mr. Winchester, we christened it, "Jimmy's Smolt," not a very clever title, but one that's easy to remember. It's a very effective, simple little pattern — one that I've been pleased to carry as one of my chosen dozen, or so, standard Alaska fly patterns ever since. It's the kind of fly a flyperson can reach for and discover results with in a hurry.

It's not much of a complex pattern, really - it's simply a size-4 hook wrapped with a thin pearl body, a sparse red tail, a sparse blue, green, and oyster flashabou wing - with a bit of sparse, bright red hackle tied in at the throat. Nevertheless, it's an absolutely deadly spring char and rainbow pattern — trust me. I've often tried the similar, smaller pattern called the Thundercreek, but without question, "Jimmy's Smolt" has always provided me with better results.

After nearly three hours of hooking and releasing char (until our wrists began to ache), we all agreed we'd had enough – for a time, at least. Jimmy's Smolt pattern had provided us with a wonderful afternoon of fly-fishing for those chunky, Alaska beauties.

Preparing to leave, I broke down my rod and stowed it in the aluminum tube, but almost before I knew it, Chris and Jimmy were talking about yet another fishing spot.

"Think we should take a look at Hightop Lake at the top of the mountain, just where it the river flows out ?" Jimmy asked.

Chris was smiling –which meant he was all for it – and Kurt and Scottie were nodding their heads, too.

"Sure, what the heck," I responded. "You're only young once, and as long as we're out here, we might as well go for at least one more stop!"

Six or seven minutes later the powerful Beaver had lugged us to the lake. Sure enough, there it was, glimmering, almost as I'd remembered it from a couple of years earlier. The only difference was, this time the beach was rimmed by a 2-foot deep snowpatch. The place looked like a picture postcard.

Discovering snow at that altitude didn't really surprise any of us, after all, it was only June 8 – still springtime in Alaska. Summer didn't officially begin until June 21, just about the exact same time the days'd begin getting shorter again.

Chris banked the floatplane around the lake's perimeter, carefully checking the wind, taking a closer look at the waves to determine their height. Only after another go around and look-see did he lower the flaps and bring the airplane in for a landing.

I frequently marvel at the flying capabilities of Alaska's bush pilots. Through experience, many of them develop the knack of spotting several very important, very key elements all at once. Often, in what appears to be one brief glance, they can ascertain many important things. In what seems like a heartbeat they can often determine the wind's direction, the height of the waves, the texture and quality of the various beaches at a lake, not to mention whether the size of the lake is sufficient for landing and for take off, and the approach path required to land the floatplane, minimizing any chance of damaging the floats – or something even more important.

For the next hour and a half we hooked and released several medium-sized rainbows at the outlet of that lake. Jimmy caught more than I did, but then again, Jimmy didn't have to spend fifteen minutes reassembling his rod, reel, line, and leader after the floatplane landed like I did.

Fifteen inches was the average, with some 'bows slightly larger. It's a uniquely beautiful location, that lake outlet, and it was even more so that day – with the snow reflecting on the surface of the ice cold lake.

A glance at our watches showed it was nearing six p.m. Time to be getting back to the floatplane for the hour and a half flight back to the lodge.

Back at Iliamna Lake Resort, Chris and I took a little time to study a large map of Alaska they keep in the main lodge. We retraced our path and were amazed to see the distance we'd covered in our explorations. It quickly became obvious that I'd been treated to at least fifteen of the area's twenty or so best fishing spots.

After dinner one evening, James (another ILR guide) asked if I'd like to grab a boat and fly-fish the Newhalen River for a couple of hours. Since the Newhalen's a particular favorite of mine, was nearby, and just happened to be the very same river that James's family has lived on for several years, my answer was obvious: "I can be wearing neoprene and be ready to go in five minutes. Is that soon enough?"

James wanted to take me just below some of the small islands in the river – to test the riffles found just below each of them. Looking at the Newhalen from it's banks, one can hardly even *see* these tiny islands, but from a boat, out on the river, they're there, all right – scattered here and there in the river's wide currents. James said he thought we might find some rainbows hanging just downstream of these tiny islands "...ready to take a fly."

I said I just might be ready to give it a try.

It just so happened I'd brought along a little bamboo fly rod with me on that trip – a used Nat Uslan, 5-strip, 2-piece, 2-tip, 7-footer that I'd picked up from my old friend, Harry Geron, down at the fly shop. It's an unusual rod that had fascinated me from the moment Harry pulled it out of its case. Before I knew it I was the proud owner of a relatively rare, used, Uslan/Feierabend, 5-

strip bamboo fly rod. No way was I not going to own that rod; *besides,* the price was right. Harry took a couple of spare fly reels I'd owned but didn't need, straight across the board. Come to think of it, though, Harry *had* been in a pretty good mood that day.

I realized that a little fly-fishing venture on the Newhalen with James might prove to be the perfect opportunity to test the new rod.

Well, maybe not perfect. Come to think of it, most people wouldn't even dream of pulling out a bamboo fly rod to fish –of all places– the Newhalen River. But I was anxious to test the new Uslan, and I was curious to see if it was going to be a lucky rod for me. Better yet, I wanted to see if I could hook a fish on my very first cast, Newhalen or no.

Our biggest advantage was that at 9:00 in the evening most of the other guides and clients would be long back at their lodges, rehashing the days' fishing.

James and I would have the Newhalen nearly to ourselves.

Besides, the very thought of fly-fishing the Newhalen (a large river by any standards) using an 'old fashioned' bamboo rod made me that much more anxious to try.

After driving the five miles or so to the river, we hopped in a boat and James motored us upstream to one of the "invisible" islands. There we climbed out, pulled the boat up on 'dry land,' and secured the anchor in the rocks.

Suprisingly, I found myself reaching for my tattered Jimmy's Smolt pattern that I'd used earlier that day for char. Instinctively, I tied it onto the 7 1/2-foot, 3X tapered leader I was using.

Usually, I would have selected either a Renegade or an Irresistible dry fly to make that first cast (I'd never even cast a smolt pattern from a cane rod before) but inherently, I knew it to be a touch too early in the season for dries just yet, especially in those big currents.

Still, I just had this *feeling*. Not only about catching fish, but particularly about the cane rod I'd just acquired. I'm fairly superstitious about new equipment, and there was just something about the feel and smell of that old rod.

Five-strip rods are fairly uncommon, and often viewed in one of two distinct ways: (1) they're absolutely adored, or (2) they're looked down upon by the 6-strip aficionados, those who feel 5-strip rods are an inferior design. I tend to disagree.

The physics of a cross section of a 5-strip (pentagon) design dictates that a joint (or seam) always opposes a "flat," whether powering forward or making a backcast. A 6-strip (hexagon) rod, on the other hand, employs another "flat" opposing each flat. This simply creates a softer, "medium" type action, which forces rod makers to add additional heft to the butt and mid-section of the rod – thus adding more weight.

Some "knowledgeable" cane fly-fishers tend to shy away from 5-strip rods like the plague. Personally, I *like* the feel of casting a 5-strip rod. In fact, I could tell I liked it from the first minute I took it out of its tattered old case and lawn-cast it. It threw a Wulff 5/6 Triangle Taper with more power than any cane rod I'd ever tested before. 5-strip rods seem to posess far more speed by offering a more rigid "backbone." *What the heck*, I thought, "as long as the thing stays glued together."

When I first acquired that rod, Harry told me I'd probably like it quite a bit. And Harry Geron, who is something of a walking fishing tackle encyclopedia, *knows* what he's talking about.

That Uslan's not an extremely attractive creation, to be sure, but somehow its old, faded, olive-lime green wrappings and the snake guide used as a hook keeper up near the cork handle make for a very unique fishing instrument, indeed.

Its tonkin strips are rather orange and they contrast nicely with the old, green guide wrappings. I rather like the simple, nickle-silver hardware that slides over the reverse-tapered, English-style cork grip. Like I say, it's a rod that's only seven feet long, but it's a nifty little fly-fishing instrument, a thing of rare beauty – to my eyes, at least.

I often wonder about used bamboo rods: Who owned it? What was he or she like? Was the rod willed to a son or a nephew after someone died? Did somebody finally give the ol' fishing pole away to the Salvation Army after it stood in the closet for several years? More importantly, *How the heck did Harry get a hold of it?*

James watched intently as I executed my first cast.

A drift, a swing, a twitch or two, and behold: Nothing.

Refusing to end the possibility of getting a strike on my very first cast, I allowed the fly to hang and tumble loosely in those currents for what seemed forever until, finally...

Nothing. Not even a smolt nibble.

Casually, then, and almost as if in slow motion, I followed with a second cast, allowing the lucky smolt pattern to tumble and drift loosely, swinging across the currents. I was just noticing it getting darker and I couldn't really see my footing as well as I. . .

Suddenly, from out of nowhere came a large, silvery flash. I remember seeing the fish as it raced up and headed for my fly. In an instant he was there and grabbed the smolt pattern and was fast to my hook!

Then the line tightened with a showery spray and my Orvis CFO III reel began to whine. I could tell immediately that this was a very respectable fish, "a fish to be reckoned with," as they say. I composed myself and tried to appear to James like this was the sort of thing I did every day.

Just another 6-pound rainbow on the 'ol bamboo, James...

Indeed, that fish turned out to be a rainbow. It was also a fighter, a solid, chunky, heavily-spotted 6-pound 'bow – a 'buck,' or male fish, a heck of a fine rainbow trout anyway you look at it.

If I remember correctly, James and I counted four very virile jumps from that rainbow in those swift currents - followed by a dogged fight before finally coming to hand.

James assisted with the photos – I had to have a photo of that fish– and after he snapped a couple, I unbuttoned the hook and released that beauty – unharmed – returning it to its familiar haunts.

"All right!!" James and I hollered nearly in unison. "Live - to fight again another day for another lucky fisherman!" The pretty, spotted rainbow soon scampered off and quickly disappeared.

For a few minutes I just stood there, breathing deeply, looking around, just taking in the beauty of the Newhalen and the sweet smell of success.

There was nary a witness, really, 'cept my guide, James, but then, who cared? I knew what had happened on that very second cast with my 35-year old used Uslan – *that* was all that mattered to me.

"That, my friend, is what fly-fishing is all about, is it not?" I said looking at James, who was grinning from ear to ear.

To say the least, I was pleased with that fish – it had not only made my day but it had made the whole trip.

As Lani Waller says in his videos, "Ya gotta believe."

Even though I was ready to call it a night (it had, after all been quite a day), James insisted on more fishing. So I continued casting, even though I couldn't have cared less if I never caught another fish.

Just for the fun of it, I changed flies to a Renegade (I'd save that smolt pattern for a spot on the office wall) and managed to hook a few small grayling and another small 'bow before it came time to call it quits for the night, even though the sun could still be seen hanging low on the horizon, reflecting off the lovely Newhalen.

James had done a admirable job of guiding that evening and had been a great fishing companion. I shall remember being out there on Alaska's Newhalen River with him for a very long time.

My stay at Iliamna Lake Resort had been exceptional. I really didn't set any records in the fish-catching department – other than numbers of char – but it *was* early in the season, yet, and I *was* beginning to work the cobwebs out and I had managed a few grayling and one particular 6-pound rainbow on a bamboo rod.

I had enjoyed the company of Jimmy, Masao, James, and Chris and the rest of the ILR staff, and I was very much aware of what a wonderful smorgasborg of fly-fishing experiences I'd had. The fishing was surpassed only by the camaraderie we shared.

I often find it ironic; somehow, after all is said and done, I always remember the people I meet at Alaska's fishing lodges much more than I do the fish – well, *most* fish, anyway.

Next morning, after breakfast, I began packing for the second leg of my fly-fishing opener. My next stop would take me across Lake Iliamna to assist with a fly-fishing video, fishing out of Bob Cusack's Alaska Lodge. It would be two more weeks before I'd return home to Anchorage and the wonderful world of advertising.

Like I carefully explained to my wife later – *some weekends are simply longer than others.*

Fly-Fishing Adventure #3
Fly-Fishing Video Days
Bob Cusack's Alaska Lodge

Tony Weaver and Mike Hood were scheduled to arrive at
Iliamna Airport on the one o'clock ERA flight from Anchorage.

If all went according to plan, they were bringing along a 2-man
video/audio team with them for the purpose of shooting a 30-
minute video segment scheduled to air sometime the coming fall on
Prime Sports Northwest.

They'd asked me to assist them in selecting a lodge over
Iliamna way and had invited me to tag along and join them for the
fishing and the taping. As I recall, it was Mike's first visit to
Iliamna country, even though he'd fished several of Alaska's other
great waters, including the famed Karluk at Kodiak. To say the
least, Big Mike was very enthusiastic about making his trip to
Iliamna. Who wouldn't be?

I'd arrived at Iliamna Airport an hour or so early, so I'd just
been standing around outside the terminal, watching the small
airplanes come and go, just killing time when the big, ERA
commercial flight from Anchorage circled and landed in a cloud of
dust. It was easy to sense the excitement in the air as I watched
the faces of the visitors as they unboarded.

Everybody was very excited, a fairly typical Iliamna reaction, really. After all, in the eyes of many, arriving at Iliamna, Alaska, does equate somewhat to finally achieving Valhalla in a sense. Heck, you could almost taste the excitment in the air.

It occurred to me that Eli would have probably liked to be there, but then again, it might have been too much for any dyed-in-the-wool fly-fishing fanatic like Eli. I could just picture him; scurrying around, shaking hands with everybody, introducing himself to all the forklift operators and the maintenance crew and asking things like, "caught any *big* fish lately?"

It *would* have been fun to watch, but after all, this *was* business. We were there to shoot a fishing video for *Prime Sports Northwest*, for heck's sakes, not go and get too excited about fly-fishing one of Alaska's great rivers.

My friend, Greg Hamm (Iliamna Bear Foot Adventures) had introduced me to Bob Cusack prior to the trip. I hadn't met Bob personally —yet— but we had talked on the phone long distance on several occasions, making plans and setting up details and the like. Bob had agreed to meet us at Iliamna's Pike Lake and help fly us across the lake over to his lodge.

Earlier that spring, Chris Goll – another Alaska fishing lodge owner – had mentioned I'd probably get a kick out of meeting Bob Cusack, so, naturally, I was very anxious to get to know this well-liked, extremely colorful Alaska lodge owner.

Bob would help transport video equipment and gear across Iliamna over to the Copper, and would house and feed the five of us for the three or four days it would require to complete the taping.

Mike and Tony would do most of the fishing segments and be ready to go when the cameras rolled. They'd do both individual *and* joint video segments. Mike would introduce the lead ins and the commercial breaks, and Tony would add the casting tips, describe various casting techniques, and advise in all the technical areas. I didn't officially have a title, so I simply acted as *support technician*, wandering around searching for rainbows...the sort of stuff that would require me to carry a fly rod with me at all times.

The venture was orginally planned to be an early season dry fly affair, but upon arrival at theriver we quickly saw that the water was flowing far too deep and swift for fishing dries just then – not exactly prime dry fly conditions any way we tried to look at it. A glance at the calendar on my watch read, June 12.

Ah! *Springtime in Alaska.*

But there was both good news and bad news, however: The good news was, the weather was cool, calm and clear - *Superb weather, actually* - save for an occasional, brief rainshower here and there in the mornings and sometimes during late afternoons. The bad news was, even though the fishing proved to be entirely acceptable, we were forced to *"go down after 'em* (rainbows) utilizing 24-foot Teeny 130's and 200's, and 25-foot Makenzie 200 grain sinktip lines. The Copper was running deeper than usual.

Not that that's *bad,* mind you.

Greg Hamm (who was guiding for Bob Cusack at the time) and local guide, Jim Tilly, (who lives and guides in that area year around and knows The Copper as well as anyone) boated us upstream from the lower mouth to a beautiful run formed just where another smaller stream enters in. It's a pretty stretch of water, just there, the kind of place a fly-fisher tends to remember for a long time after the fishing has ended.

I remembered that stretch of water. I'd fished that same, pretty confluence on a couple of different occasions in the past – both with Greg Hamm, and with Dennis McCracken – and had pulled out more than a few nice fish from that same hole.

One, an eight pound rainbow had given me a deep, twisting battle I'll long remember, and another, a five and a half pounder, turned out to be a real jumper, unusual for a fish that large. Both rainbows were taken on a floating line, employing a long leader – *nymphing* a single egg pattern as they call it.

Roger Miller of VisuArt Productions in Anchorage served as lead camerman, while Rob Hood (no relation to Mike) assisted with the sound equipment and with selecting additional camera angles.

As Roger set up the camera and Rob rigged the long, extended microphone, Tony and Mike and I assembled our tackle and began fishing. With the high water we faced, our first objective proved to be selecting the correct sink tip line to get us down to where we hoped the rainbows would be. I say hoped because, *even on the Copper,* there are no guarantees.

Teeny T-200? Teeny T-130?

Occasionally, another lodge boat would come by, temporarily disrupting the filming, but for the most part the video taping went well. I wandered downstream (like any good *support technician* is supposed to do) and fished for a half hour or so while Tony and Mike got set up and shook the cobwebs out.

Big Mike's a very decent fly-fisherman, the type I call a *natural*, the type who's not afraid to wade out in deep water and fish hard to seams and confluences. After selecting a choice piece of water in front of the camera, Mike quickly hooked into one nice rainbow, and then another. Roger and Rob had to get the camera and sound gear rolling quickly before Mike's hot hands cooled off.

Ten minutes later, downstream 100 yards, after switching from a T-130 to a T-200 (you've got to fish at the right depth, *Danny Boy*) my sculpin pattern finally began heating up, too. In the next couple of minutes I hooked and released two nice, densely spotted, 22 inch rainbows. The skies had sprinkled us with a mild rainshower for a minute or two just then and the fishing got really hot in a hurry. Naturally, we released all of our fish –unharmed.

One of those 'bows provided me with *seven* superb jumps – *I know, I counted 'em* – before I managed to bring it to hand for unbuttoning. Bob Cusack seemed to be having the time of his life running around with his video camera, busy trying out his new camcorder (with a waterproof housing attached) and achieved some exciting closeup underwater footage of rainbows being caught and released.

One evening, after fishing a long run, Greg Hamm guided us downstream to a lovely spot set along a steep rock cliff – a superb dry fly flow where Mike quickly hopped out, stripped a big mouse pattern across the surface, and hooked a 16 incher in the process. It was exciting to watch, although it happened so fast that I'm not sure the cameras were rolling at the time.

Naturally, the rest of us scurried to tie on dry flies as fast as our fingers would turn clinch knots and began casting. Ironically, in the end, it was assistant camerman Rob Hood who stole the show by hooking his very first rainbow, ever, on a fly rod; a fine, 15-inch hen taken right at the surface, using a size-12 Royal Wulff.

It's always great fun to hook rainbows on dry flies, but to be standing next to an angler who has just experienced his first fish (especially when it's a fine, spotted rainbow that gives-up three or four worthy jumps as this one had) is classic stuff – even better when it happens on a classic dry fly.

That particular spot is a lovely one, a deep, smooth glide where slow, swirling water meanders gently alongside a sharp, rugged outcrop. It's a place where Alaska spruce trees frame a perfect Alaska fly-fishing setting, especially where they reflect off the river's glassy surface. I'm thinking maybe I'll try and go back to that spot one of these first days – maybe some evening around eight o'clock – just me and my guide, and maybe a bamboo fly rod, all strung up and ready to go with maybe a big, furry Stimulator.

Our stay at Cusack's Alaska Lodge proved to be very entertaining, enlightening, and exceptionally scenic. The fishing, considering the high water we faced, still proved to be good.

By the way, a visit to Bob Cusack's Alaska Lodge is a grand Alaska lodge experience, one where guests enjoy superb, gourmet cuisine and laugh at the stories of a man who has logged thousands of hours adventuring all across the state – both fishing and hunting.

Bob Cusack's is an immaculate, intimate lodge, designed to comfortably house eight to ten guests, overlooking a very picturesque cove in a very secluded Iliamna bay. The lodge is located just minutes from the currents of the beautiful Copper, in a panoramic setting which isn't bothered much by competing traffic. The lodge presently operates a Cessna-182, a Cessna-185, a Cessna-206, and a Piper Super Cub, each on floats.

Those who come to know him quickly learn that Bob Cusack is an exceedingly colorful, extremely experienced, resourceful individual, a master big game guide who has spent many years guiding both hunters and fishermen all across the state. Bob Cusack knows much of Alaska like the back of his hand.

For several years back in the seventies, Bob operated a fishing camp from a floating barge (houseboat) over on the Alagnak (Branch) River - "almost before anyone else even knew that king salmon are to be found there," he says.

"It *was back* in the early seventies and I had the river nearly all to myself for approximately seven or eight years," Bob recalls today, "but eventually, I began to notice the Kakhonak area over here at Iliamna and I decided to build myself a permanent lodge." Bob says.

"I still guide moose, bear, and caribou hunters in various parts of the state, but during fishing season I'm concentrating more and more on fly-fishers these days, mostly because of the quality of the anglers that fly-fishing attracts and the quality of the river near my lodge." All in all "...it has been a very happy evolution for *Bob Cusack's Alaska Lodge* over the past decade." Bob says.

At noon on our third day, Buster "Cajun" Patin, a pilot from Tony Sarp's KATMAI LODGE, radioed from the Beaver informing us that he'd spotted Cusack's Lodge and was ready to land in the bay. Tony Weaver was to have accompanied me on this, the third leg of my June fly-fishing opener, but Tony had to decline at the last minute because of 'other responsibilities' back in Anchorage.

I understood. *Somebody* had to go back to the city and distribute fishing tackle to flyshops and sporting goods dealers. After all, it *was* the height of fishing season, and besides, in another week, or so, Tony'd be heading out again, himself.

So, waiving goodbye to Bob Cusack and the others I climbed in the Beaver alongside Buster, headed for the Alagnak. Somebody had to go show Tony Sarp how to fish the *Braids* before responsibilities back in the city beckoned him, once again, too.

Fly-Fishing Adventure #4

Tony Sarp's KATMAI LODGE
Dry Fly-Fishing the Braids

I had looked forward to fishing *The Braids* of the Branch (or Alagnak) River all of the previous winter. Now, suddenly, all that stood between me and the rainbows and grayling on dry flies was a 55-minute bushplane flight and a little more suspected high water. I certainly wasn't wishing for high water but I half expected it.

Even though the fishing at the Copper the previous week had been excellent, high water conditions *had* caused us to have to work a bit for our fish. Well, maybe work isn't really the best way to describe it - it's just that deep, swift water *does* make for more difficult footing and fishing than is normally experienced.

Wading in high water conditions isn't always what I'd describe as being a *pleasant* endeavor. It's not that I'd rather be back in the city – don't get me wrong – but sometimes it seems it's about all one can do to maintain one's footing. *Not* drowning crosses the fly-fisher's mind somewhere along the line, and *not* getting 'bobbed' downstream in an out of control, stiff legged manner becomes a primary concern, too.

Like most fly-fishers, I don't mind a *touch* of embarrassment once in a while – everybody slips and falls in sooner or later – but please, dear fly-fishing gods, couldn't I fly-fish Alaska for just a little while longer before I actually go and *drown* myself?

I'll long remember the afternoon at the Copper that I found myself shouting for the attentions of a nearby guide. It was *really* embarrassing, but then, I *needed* him.

"A, *Excuse me...a....'ol chap, but would you mind ever so much just hurrying down here and saving my life for just a minute or two? ... that is, if you could spare me just a few moments of your time...*"

There're no two ways about it: Fishing 'new' water all the time *does* have its disadvantages. Where else (other than duck or goose hunting) can a sportsman go out and risk his life to unexpected deep, or surprisingly swift water all in the name of *sport?*

How was I supposed to know it's ten feet deep down there? Everybody knows the Copper isn't *that* deep....*IS IT?*"

Now, suddenly, I was sitting next to Buster in Tony Sarp's newly remodeled deHavilland Beaver, on my way to the Branch. It had been four years and several rivers since I'd fished Alaska's famed Alagnak, and it was good to view that big, broad, Branch River Valley once again. I always find myself enjoying scanning over endless miles of rolling Alaska tundra over the purr of a cruising bushplane.

I'd *seen* Buster 'Cajun' Patin earlier in my travels –somewhere– but I'd never had the pleasure of meeting him before. Our flight from Kakhonak at Iliamna to the Branch offered Buster and me the chance to get to know each other better.

As we flew along I couldn't help but reflect on how fortunate I was to be on my way to yet another of Alaska's premier fishing lodges. Like I say, it was especially exciting to be returning to the famed Alagnak, a river that is very significant to me since it not only ranks as one of Alaska's very best, but it was the river that served as my final opportunity of fly-fishing with my father. And the wild Alagnak is as wild and *Alaskan* as they come. If I give the impression that I *like* the Branch, you're right. In fact, I'd be hard pressed to choose three favorite fly-fishing waters in Alaska *without* including the Alagnak.

"I'll give you *both* the such and such *and* the so and so – but *I'll* take the Alagnak, okay?

Tony Sarp's new pilot turned out to be experienced in Alaska, a man who still speaks with a very distinct, Mississippian drawl. Buster's a very personable fellow, a real gentleman, but what I like about him most, is, Buster flies *by the book*. Somehow, I've always admired that particular attribute in Alaska's bush pilots.

Tony Sarp's pretty, newly refurbished, yellow and blue deHavilland Beaver is a real beauty – a Kenmore refurbished model if I'm not mistaken, a sweetheart of an airplane that was only recently acquired from a wealthy entrepreneur in Anchorage who had two of 'em and couldn't how to fly 'em both at the same time.

Our flight to Katmai Lodge –located on the steep banks of the *Branch*– took us over some extremely remote tundra scenery. Buster and I'd flown for only fifteen or seventeen minutes when I realized the last habitation we'd noticed was the native village of Kakhonak, located several miles behind us on the southerly shores of giant Lake Iliamna. It was *wild* country below.

As we approached the big, winding Alagnak, off in the distance we could see the mighty Kvichak (Kwee-jack) River (the outlet of Iliamna) to the north. Once again I felt the excitement of being in Alaska's premier Bristol Bay region. I'd learned several years earlier what a marvelous fishery the Alagnak is, and the fact that I was headed there now, expressly for the purpose of floating dry flies on the famous *braids*, only made my adrenalin pump that much harder.

Finally, we approached the river, and with the Branch flowing directly beneath us, at my request, Buster backed-off on the throttle, lowering our elevation slightly. This allowed me an extra close look at *The Braids*. What a grand sight these broken ribbons of river make. Glancing upstream a few miles, I could just make out where the two main tributaries (Kukaklek and Nonvianuk) come together, forming *a 'Branch'* in the river. Turning back toward Katmai Lodge, Buster applied throttle, climbing back up to cruising altitude. Our destination, Tony Sarp's KATMAI LODGE, was just barely visible in the distance.

There's something truly wild and remote about Alaska's Alagnak river country, something fairly difficult to describe, especially to those who haven't experienced it for their first time. Possibly it's because the river is located just far enough away from any of the other major drainages in that region of Alaska – whatever, I always think of the place as, 'Wild Alaska River Country.'

But there was *one*sure thing that I remembered about the Alagnak that I'd learned earlier: The Alagnak River *is most definitely* home to some of the most gorgeous, heavily spotted rainbow trout in all of the Great Land. I've yet to decide if it's because of Lake Nonvianuk's influence *or* that of Lake Kukalek's, but one thing's for certain: the Branch River system is undoubtedly home to some of the premier rainbow trout fishing in all of Alaska.

As KATMAI LODGE came into clearer view I was amazed at the size of the camp and the numbers of buildings. It had been four years, or so, since I'd first seen the place, and out front, down at the river, workers could be seen constructing a high retaining wall in an effort to restrict the amount of continuous bank erosion.

It occurred to me that Eli would have enjoyed this trip, also. Too bad he'd had to stay in Anchorage and move furniture.

Buster executed another of his, 'Textbook Landings,' and he and I were met at the dock by something like fifteen or twenty of the lodge's guides and dock hands including one smiling Lodge Manager named Lester Jacober. Buster carefully taxiied the big, yellow floatplane up to the lodge's floating ramp where he cut the engine and we drifted the last few feet to the dock.

It was easy to see the enthusiasm in the eyes of the guides and others who'd crowded to greet us. Like myself, they, too, were happy to be out on one of Alaska's ultimate fly-fishing rivers – but no happier than I was.

Les introduced me to several of the lodge's guides and showed me to a warm, comfortable room upstairs in one of the six or seven large guest buildings built right alongside theAlagnak. My room was located upstairs in a newly-constructed, two-story building named *"Brown Bear."*

"Would you like to go out with Ray Johnson for a few hours of fly-fishing before dinner? Lester asked, as he helped me with my bags and gear.

"Heck, Yes! !" I responded, "....that sounds like a splendid idea, a very splendid idea, indeed, for a Sunday afternoon on the Alagnak. *Thank You Very Much – YES!"* I replied.

It was hell having to climb off a floatplane and then having to jump into a riverboat and go speeding off to one of Alaska's ultimate rivers to fly-fish for twelve pound rainbow trout–*but somebody had to do it.*

"I can be in my waders and be down at the dock in twenty minutes!" I said to Les. Sixteen minutes later I was down at the dock, my 6-weight graphite fly rod and my Hardy Marquise-6 fly reel in hand, where Katmai Lodge guide, Ray Johnson was warming up the boat. Fifteen minutes later Ray pulled in to an island, where we got out on foot and anchored the boat.

Both Ray and I'd survived downpours in the past, but neither of us had ever experienced anything like the thunderstorm that rolled through that river valley the next hour. We'd only barely arrived when the skies suddenly darkned and a huge thundercloud came likety split. It looked like wizard of oz time.

I remember, I'd barely hooked, played, and released a 23-inch rainbow (using a big, fluffy, size-2 dark sculpin pattern of Ray's manufacture) when rain and hail began falling on us like neither of us had ever witnessed before in our lives. Within a minute both of us were totally soaked before either of us could dawn our raingear. Within a couple of minutes the surrounding grasses and bushes at streamside were severly beaten down by the storm, which lasted a mere four or five minutes before it ended as suddenly as it had begun.

Unlike the Rocky Mountain west, for some strange reason, Alaska doesn't get too many of these sudden thunderstorms. But this particular storm had ranked with any I'd ever experienced. We pitied any pilots who might have been airborne when that awesome thunderhead rolled through.

After the storm subsided Ray guided me to some of his favorite spots where I was able to hook into three or four more heavily spotted 'bows just like the first - *not bad* for a couple of hours of fly-fishing, especially when I stopped to realize that some anglers never experience a true 24-inch rainbow trout in their entire lives. Ironically, here I was, calling that afternoon's fishing *'fairly decent'* with four or five 24-inchers in just a couple of hours.

Those rainbows would grab those big, black and purple sculpins right on the swing, just as the fly would come to the point where it would begin a sideways motion across the currents. The theory is, that the fish start to 'think' the strange 'food item' is beginning to get away from them – *sounds like a good theory to me.*

During the next couple of days I had the pleasure of meeting and fishing with Amato Publications' writer Bill Herzog, and his companion, Mike Cronen, both super guys who hail from the Oregon and Washington areas.

Bill's an editor for STS (Salmon-Trout-Steelheader magazine) and both men turned out to be very knowledgeable, experienced

anglers, indeed, *Steelheaders par Excellence* as they say, with
many hundreds of hours of trophy fishing under each of their
belts. I quickly began to see that both of these two men deserved
spots among the best anglers I'd ever fished with.

Later that night, Mike graciously showed me some of the
pictures he'd taken from previous steelhead expeditions. To say
the least, the fish these two men had caught and released over the
years were impressive. Both these guys had learned the art of
reading water. They were obviously both anglers who live to fish,
both living proof that experience breeds success. It was great
fishing with Bill and Mike, easy to see the strong friendship they'd
developed over the years.

Depending upon the fish specie/s an angler wishes to pursue
(and the time of season and the particular salmon run in progress)
anglers may travel up, or downstream from Katmai Lodge, which is
situated very near the halfway point on the river.

Downstream, The Alagnak runs deep and wide, and finding
flats here and there along the lower river is generally where much
of the great king and chum salmon fishing is to be found.
Upstream, particularly in the *Braids*, is where the river's ultimate
rainbow, silver, and grayling fishing is located.

Since we were specifically in pursuit of rainbow trout, all of
our fishing occurred upstream of the lodge, and a fleet of several
modern jet boats was assigned to the task. In all instances, each of
these boats were captained by an experienced, very qualified river
guide at the helm. One of the many interesting things I discovered
about the Katmai Lodge operation is that each boat at the lodge is

assigned to a particular section of the river - therefore, competition from other boats from the lodge is never a problem. If an angler was to request that he's desiring rainbow fishing on dry flies, for example, that angler would simply be assigned to a boat which will travel to the appropriate section of the river. Head Guide, Tom Haugen, (with several years of experience on the *Branch*) guides on the river and also manages duties at the lodge, while Bob (Bobcat) Schierholz, along with Lodge Manager Les Jacober, combine to coordinate ground operations.

Bobcat's an expert flytier, and afterhours, guests can turn to him for assistance and advice when it comes time to create some 'killer' patterns' for the next days' fishing. Frans Jensen is another of Katmai Lodges' several master guides who's also logged several years of Alagnak River experience. One of the interesting things I learned on this trip was that, a few years earlier, Frans had placed something like second or third in a World Fly-Casting Tournament. Of course, you'd never know that from talking to Frans, I just happened to hear that tid bit of information from somebody else.

Being a dry fly fisherman at heart, it was with open arms that I witnessed a vigorous caddis fly hatch occuring the following day on *The Braids*.

We'd just pulled up to a small island and anchored the baot. I was just sitting there, had just placed down my rod and reel, ready to grab a diet cola when, all of a sudden, a huge insect hatch – looking much like a snowstorm in December – began. Naturally, lunch could wait. Now it was time to do what we'd come for!

Within minutes it looked as if it was snowing all around us. I'd heard about (but had never witnessed) such a magnificent hatch ever before in my life. Yet, somehow I wasn't too surprised. *After all,* I'm never surprised about The Alagnak anymore; it's simply one of the most fertile rainbow and grayling fisheries in all of Alaska. *'This might not be heaven,* I thought, but *it did* cause me to reach for my dry fly box in record time.

The bugs were flying!

Instinctively, we all scrambled from the boat and began moving into position in the currents. After grabbing my 9-foot, Loomis 5-weight, I quickly tied on a Renegade.

Irresistibles and Stimulators both proved to work extremely well, too, but I grabbed a Renegade soley out of belief in the fly, even though I realized I should probably be tying-on an Elk Hair Caddis.

Suddenly we found ourselves standing in a dry fly fisherman's heaven, like I say, by far and away the finest dry-fly hatch I'd ever expeienced in my life.

'If only my wife could see me now – *then* she'd understand...."
I thought.

Soon we were able to gain the attentions of several of the good-sized grayling we found surfacing all around us, and every once in a while someone would manage to hook one of those beautiful spotted rainbow trout that seem to lie in wait *just behind* the grayling. We must have landed and released seventy-five grayling and twenty-five rainbows between us during the next couple of hours.

The next morning it was Bill Herzog who found himself with the hot hands and the hot fly. I noticed that Bill was fishing a fairly light, 9-foot, 5-weight fly rod, employing the talents of a big, ugly, fluffy, black and purple sculpin pattern. I noticed that Bill was using a Teeny T-200, quick-sinking 24-foot sinktip line.

Bill had said it had been a lucky fly and combination for him the previous few days, but this, our third day, seemed better yet. Sometimes it's surprising how one angler can suddenly 'feel the magic,' and it was definitely Bill Herzog who turned out to be the lucky angler *this* morning. Bill wasted no time locating a prime flow, hooking into a beautiful, 28 1/2 inch, ten or eleven pound, heavily spotted rainbow trout hen that looked to be the very same shape as a summer run steelhead. Ironically, Bill had hooked that fish on the same magical (if ugly) purple and black sculpin pattern he'd been using all week. I offered to buy that fly from him, but, '*no dice.*'

Suddenly it dawned on me I'd fallen into the old trap of merely going through *the motions* in my fishing. All fly-fishers fall into this trap sooner or later, but I had to admit; I *had* become lazy and *had* done a fairly poor job of attempting to read water of late. Maybe I was growing physically tired after such an extended fly-fishing oddessy, but if I was going to be out there fishin', I might as well *fish* I decided. I wasn't fishing very 'smart.' Any angler who has any experience astream at all will know what I'm talking about here; it's a sort of mental hole that an angler can suddenly find himself in - a condition that 'sneaks in' every so often if we're not careful. As much as it hurt my personal ego, I decided to make a permanent point of either 'paying attention to the fishing' or going back to the room at the lodge and flipping through fly-fishing magazines. After all, I reasoned, if one is going to fly-fish, doesn't he owe it to himself to fish the best waters around him?

I made it a point to get a full ten full hours sleep that night.

During my 5 days at Katmai Lodge The Alagnak proved to be a wonderful fishery, as usual. It was still as good as I'd remembered it from my earlier experiences. It's an ultimate rainbow and arctic grayling destination, *The Branch,* just as it's also a salmon angler's utopia. One thing was for certain: Tony Sarp's KATMAI LODGE had lived up to it's reputation as being one of Alaska's very finest.

Almost before I knew it, it became time for the final leg of my June fly-fishing venture, a 4-day visit to Wood River Lodge situated on the Agulawok River in the Wood River/Tikchik Lakes system of western Alaska.

Bill and Mike were headed upstream that day, headed for the outlet of Kukaklek Lake, so after waiving them goodbye and thanking Tony Sarp, Les Jacober, and the rest of the staff at Katmai Lodge, I finished packing my gear.

I found myself down at the dock with a few minutes to spare – with a chance to look around and appreciate the Alagnak and Katmai Lodge. As I waited for J.J. to arrive in the Beaver, I was impressed by the incredible lodge Tony Sarp has created in a very wilderness setting. Across the river two trumpeter swans reflected from the river's surface, and a minute later, a cow moose peered at me through some alders. Suddenly I was reminded once again how lucky I am to be at a fly-fisher in this awesome, magical land they call Alaska, and how enjoyable my stay at Katmai Lodge had been.

Fly-Fishing Adventure #5

Wood River Rendezvous
Deep In The Heart of Heaven

After circling the Alagnak three or four times before landing, suddenly, there was my old friend, J.J. Ortman – grinning from the cockpit of his big, loud, dark red de Havilland Beaver. J.J. loves Alaska – and his smile always reminds me of a kid who'd just borrowed his dad's oldsmobile without having gained permission.

J.J.'d never landed on the *Branch* before, so his circlings had given him a chance to survey the area closely and look the river over for impediments before plopping 'er down for a landing.

Smart. *Very Smart.*

J.J.'s brother, Bernie Ortman, also has a beaver similar to J.J.'s, but if I remember correctly, Bernie's is painted white with a red trim - while J.J.'s is a red airplane with a *white* trim. Actually, I have a hard time keeping the two Beavers straight. About the only way I can tell them apart on a regular basis is that Bernie's is the floatplane that has, "CHECK GAS DUMMY" scrtached into the paint on his 'firewall.' J.J. hasn't come up with *his* masterpiece slogan, yet – maybe he's still thinking of something to top Bernie.

It had been a couple of years since I'd had the pleasure of seeing J.J.'s wide grin (J.J.'s the abbreviated name I use to refer to Mr. John Ortman, Jr.). J.J.'s the kind of Alaska Lodge owner who's *always* smiling, it seems, but then, come to think of it, Les Jacober at Tony Sarp's KATMAI LODGE always smiles a lot, too. Apparently, several of these guys are very happy doing what they're doing – busy running very professional , top of the line Alaska fishing lodges.

'Why isn't advertising like that, Eli?"

As J.J. idled over to the dock, over the rumble of his engine I shouted things like, "*Want a cup of coffee?*" "*Do you need to use the restroom?*" and "*How's that crazy brother of yours doing?*"

As always, J.J.'s answers came short and to the point:

"Nope. Thanks anyway, Don't need no coffee, Don't need a bathroom, and, Yup, Bernie's still as crazy as ever! *Hop in!*"

"*Let's get airborne* and get out of this dreaded Katmai weather and get over to the Tikchiks where the sun is *always* shining!" J.J. teased.

J.J. was right. We'd had great weather at Katmai Lodge for the past four days, but today's weather was.....*well*....

"I'm ready to fly whenever you are, *Doctor*" I said as I latched the front door of the Beaver and reached for my shoulder harness.

"*Let 'er Rip...Doc!* I'm ready to cheat death one more time if you are - *and by the way*, thanks a lot for comin' and fetchin' me, and if you need any advice on how to fly this thing, don't hesitate to ask; call Bernie, *okay?!*"

Now, suddenly, it was time for leg four of my June fly-fishing oddessy. Presently we were taxiing as J.J. made the final adjustements on the flaps for takeoff.

"We're Off!," J.J. shouted as he pressed forward on the throttle, one of three long levers sticking up on the Beaver's dashboard. "You work these other two levers, whatever they are, *and I'll watch the throttle*, J.J. teased, causing the airplane to shake and rumble. Then, suddenly, we were airborne.

Quickly the big floatplane lifted off, powering up, over the cottonwoods - the mighty Alagnak River now appearing much smaller down below us than it is in reality.

At about 600 feet J.J. leveled off. The big, loud, radial engine was purring at about 1800 R.P.M.'s as J.J. headed the floatplane in a west/southwest direction.

From earlier trips to Wood River / Tikchik country I knew we were headed for the beautiful rolling tundra country that gently works it's way up the hills to the panoramic Tikchik Mountain range, located about an hour and a half distant. Once there, we'd be smack dab in the middle of what they refer to as western Alaska– and smack dab in the middle of some of the most fantastic dry fly fishing I've ever expperienced.

J.J. and I had a chance to renew our old aquaintance as we flew. Minor changes had occurred in both of our lives and it was good to have a few minutes alone with Junior. A couple of years earlier J.J. had been the pilot who'd flown over in a Cessna-185 from Wood River Lodge to pick up John Gierach, DeWitt Daggett, and me at Quinnat Landing Hotel on the banks of the Naknek River in King Salmon. What followed was a fantastic five day dry fly-fishing adventure – my first taste of the wonders of the Tikchik Lakes System and incredible Wood River Lodge.

J.J. treated us to some spectacular wildlife viewing during that flight – which included a fairly-close look at a perfectly blonde brown bear sow and her two perfectly blonde first year cubs. We also spotted numerous moose and bands of scattered caribou here and there along those hillsides that work their way from rolling tundras up to the pretty, Muklung Hills guarding the Tikchik Lakes. Following that flight, Mr. Gierach had commented on what an impression that air journey had made on him, and he later wrote about that trip in his book, *Dances With Trout*, in his *Alaska* chapter. (Simon and Schuster, 1994).

Fortunately, the weather only seemed to improve as our flight continued. Talk ranged everything from, "How's the fishin' out your way, to "How're the kids and the wife?" I would have taken control and flown the Beaver 'cept J.J. appeared to be doing an adequate job.

Eventually, after a very picturesque plane ride, J.J. and I wound our way throught the mountains to lovely, panoramic Lake Nerka and the Agulawok River.

Buzzing the lodge, it soon became apparent that the 'Wok was also running high - *just like* the Alagnak had been, *along with* the Copper, *and* the American, *and* Grosvenor, *and* the other Nonvianuk streams had been.

"What had happened *statewide* to cause such high water everywhere, J.J.?" I asked.

"*Late spring rains* caused an accentuated melt, spurred by an extremely warm spring runoff. Also, a late season snowfall assisted in causing higher than normal water levels," he said matter of factly.

Down at the river I could see where now, little or *no* beach existed. Two years earlier there'd been a nice riverbank.

"Darn," I rationalized, *"we'll just have to cast our dry flies from drifting boats. We'll get those rainbows yet, just wait and see!"*

My partner on this leg was Paul D. 'Eli' Rotkis, a dear friend (and a fly-fishing fanatic) who'd arrived earlier that afternoon via commercial airliner, flying to Dillingham from Anchorage. Earlier that morning, J.J. and Mrs. Linda Ortman had flown over to Dillingham to fetch Eli in a Beaver.

Eli's an experienced and extremely enthusiastic flyrodder - a fly-fisher who's probably had more experience fishing along Alaska's road systems than any other individual I know. Eli *lives* fly-fishing 365 days a year – whether he's home tying flies, at work (as a fireman) tying flies after hours, or at his part time job where he works as a customer service rep at one of Anchorage's finest sporting goods dealers. If ever there was an individual worthy for a award for *enthusiastic fly-fisher of the world,* in my book, Paul David 'Eli' Rotkis would be the recipient.

People just call him Eli.

It was exciting for us to see the beam in Eli's eyes as he explained the fishing success he'd already experienced that day before J.J. and I 'd arrived from Branch River country. This was Eli's first trip to *'the real Alaska,'* his first opportunity at fishing away from southcentral. To put it mildly, he seemed more than a little like the proverbial *kid in a candy store* after tasting of Alaska's Tikchik Lakes Region for his first time.

Suddenly, another voice joined-in the conversation, a voice much raspier than any of the other's had been. Suddenly there *he* was, standing there in the flesh – none other than Mr. Bernie K. Ortman, *himself* – J.J.'s older-looking but younger brother.

You'd have to know Bernie Ortman personally to appreciate him, he's a unique individual. Like J.J. , Bernie's also a very experienced Alaska pilot and guide, but you'd never know it by the way he acts; he's as fun loving as they come, and he has a way with making strangers feel right at home.

"How ya doin, Danny ol boy?" Bernie's voice barked. "Paul, here, has already caught himself all of the fish in the entire county while you and Johnny were off making your little cross country flight this afternoon!"

It was great to be standing there talking Bernie Ortman once again. Bernie tries to come on like a bulldog - yet he's such a mild character underneath it all that he simply has no bite - unless, of course, there's justified reason. Try as he may to be gruff, truth is, Bernie Ortman is one of the gentlest individuals I've ever had the pleasure of meeting. Like the pilot I'd met earlier who'd known Bernie for years had told me, "Bernie's more than unique– *he's a work of art.*"

Granted, Bernie Ortman *does* come on like a captain on a whaling ship every now and then, but the twinkle in his eye quickly gives away his 'tough act' which is accentuated just to get more of a reaction and a laugh out of people. Then, when the gig is up, it's usually followed by a fit of Bernie's howling laughter.

Made you laugh, *didn't I!!*

But Bernie Ortman *isn't* crazy - nor does he do dangerous things. In fact, quite the contrary: I've noticed that he goes out of his way to practice safety at all times – especially while operating an aircraft – even though he likes to tease around a little that he doesn't know how to fly the bird. A typical trick of his is to wait until everyone gets seated in his Beaver, then, climbing in a minute later he'll scratch his head, wrinkle his brow, and turn to the passengers and say, "anyone here ever *fly* one of these things before? *Jeeze*, so many switches and levers and gauges, oh, well....I guess everything looks the way it ought to be! Maybe I'll flip *this* switch and see if *it* does anything!"

When the the engine coughs and sputters and the propellor catches and turns over, the floatplane suddenly lurches forward on the water. Now that there's no turning back, that's when Bernie will likely turn again to his passengers and mutter something like, "...well, I guess we pretty well *got* to see if this thing can fly, *now*."

The irony is, Bernie Ortman has racked-up thousands of hours as an experienced Alaska bush pilot, and in all that time he's never had a moment's trouble.

Knock on wood.

Compared to Bernie, his brother, J.J. is a saint. But don't go counting out J.J. as being a prankster on occasion, too. No way. In fact, Bernie Ortman probably didn't become 'crazy' all by himself. Something tells me his older brother, J.J. Ortman, had more than a little influence on Bernie while they were growing up. Still, having a good time just seems to run in the Ortman family. *Not a bad philosophy when you stop and think about it.*

J.J.'s the kind of fellow who'll dupe you into showing him how to cast a fly line - and then proceed to demonstrate a perfectly timed, tight looped cast, just as if he's actually executing one for the first time in his life. Actually, J.J. and Bernie Ortman remind me more than a little of the Smothers Brothers: People like to think of the one brother as being crazy, but don't count out the other one as being completely capable, too.

The Ortmans share a strong sense of unity. Once, while a group of us were outside the lodge just talking and joking - J.J. and Bernie simultaneously raised a finger to their lips for all of us to stop and listen. Ever so quietly, we strained to hear what it was they were listening for.

Apparently, their father, John Ortman, Sr. was flying up from the lower-48 that day in his Cessna-185. Sure enough, a minute or two later, here came Papa John Ortman Sr., flying between the mountain pass, buzzing the lodge in that beautiful red and white floatplane of his. A second later he flared up and out, over the lodge, climbing up for his final turn and approach.

In his own inimitable style, Bernie took occasion to mutter,

"Looks like we'd better give pops a check-ride one of these first days, J.J." Bernie said.

A minute later Papa John (the man with thousands of hours as a commercial airlines pilot) appeared again, extending the 185's flaps, slowing the airplane down for a picture perfect landing on Lake Nerka.

Flying and airplanes seem to run in the Ortman family.

It wasn't long before J.J. and Bernie introduced Eli and me to a couple of their accomplished fishing guides, Mr. Greg Liu, and Mr.

Logan Ricketts, both expert fly-fishers, and both seasoned guides with several years experience between them. I was pleased to learn that Greg Liu's father, Mr. Alan Liu, is the one and the same Alan Liu that operates a fine, used fly and fishing tackle business back in Amawalk, New York. I'd seen Alan Liu's ads and articles here in there in various fishing publications over the years.

A westerner, Logan Ricketts is a skiing and fly-fishing aficionado who has lived in Whitefish, Montana as well as residing in Fairbanks, Alaska. Logan reminds me a lot of a rodeo cowboy, and he exhibits a definite western air about him. In fact, one of Logan's favorite and frequent sayings (whenever a client would hook a fish) was, *'Ya.Hoo...Everybody Ropes...and Everybody Rides!"* It always brings a smile to those around him.

It quickly became obvious that Eli had already discovered *'The Honey Hole'* down at the river out in front of the lodge. They call it by that name because of the large char (by the hundreds) and several finning grayling *-along with intriguing numbers of rainbow trout-* that continuously hang out in that area of the river. It's an easy hole to spot, really - all one has to do is walk along the path from the lodge down to the river. A typical newcommer's reaction is,....."Oh, My goodness! Just *look* at all those fish!"

Indeed.

For some strange reason Eli spent more than a fair amount of his time after dinner in the evenings fishing down at the river.

Eli and I were treated to a variety of premier fly-fishing challenges at Wood River Lodge. Fortunately, the weather was near perfect for us during our four day stay, despite the deep water that year.

One morning was spent fly-fishing from an anchored boat at a lovely little feeder stream on Lake Nerka. We fished for char, experiencing continuous hookups until nearly noon, and then, after lunch, we motored across to the upper end of the lake and fished for northern pike. Mouse patterns at the surface brought decent results, but when Eli suggested we begin using sunken *Lefty's Deceiver* patterns, the pike fishing got really hot. Later that afternoon we fished dry flies –size 10 stimulators mostly– for rainbows and grayling back on the Augulwok out in front of the lodge, gladly repeating the process again after supper. Guide Wayne Saurey was my personal dry-fly guide at the Agulawok - while Logan and Eli teamed up in a friendly competition, drifting and fishing from another boat.

Next morning, after breakfast, Bernie invited Eli, guide Greg Liu, his fiancee, Colleen, and myself on a fly-out to a pristine, little-known dry fly stream that no one seemed to know the name of. At least no one wanted to spend much time talking about its' name. *That was okay* – Eli and I understand things like that.

It's a surreal little stream situated at the outlet of one of the many lakes in the Tikchik area. When my eyes caught a glimpse of it's beginnings, just where it originates at the upper lake, I knew we were in for a grand day of dry fly-fishing.

As we circled the area we gazed down at numbers of visible (very sizeable) rainbows finning in the stream's lower currents. Back up at the top, just where the stream forms at the upper lake is where Bernie dropped us off.

"This should be a dandy of a day trip for you fellas" Bernie said smiling, looking directly at Colleen. Quickly, the four of us unloaded our rods and gear from the Beaver. Colleen might have come back with something right about then, but apparently she either didn't notice Bernie's comment or simply elected not to tackle it just then, I'm not sure which. More than likely, she'd wait until later that evening – back at the lodge at the dinner table.

Then Bernie announced, "Just take yer' time and don't mind the odor of that smelly ol' bear. It's obviously killed a moose nearby and is probably looking us over right this very instant from over there in them bushes" he said, pointing.

Bernie was right: There *Was* a terrible, awful, putrid stink in the air all around us – an offensive odor far different than the clean smell of Alaska's spruce forests one normally scents in such pictureqsque settings as this. The entire area around us *definitely* smelled of rotten carrion and of a brown bear that needed a bath.

The more we whiffed it the more we agreed with Bernie's conclusion: there definitely *was* rotten bear's scent in the air all around us – and none of us *fellas* found it surprising whatsoever when the four of us *fellas* managed to fish our way rather quickly past that spot and around the bend.

A few minutes later we could hear Bernie starting the motor of his Beaver. Then we waived as he buzzed over us on his way back to the lodge. Bernie wished us good luck by tipping his wings as he flew over, his tie-down ropes flapping behind the floatplane in the breeze.

It wasn't long before each of us started picking up small rainbows on dry flies. Occasionally I'd look over at Colleen whenever she'd hook a fish (which was quite often) and just for fun of it say,

"Nice Fish, *Fella.*"

Those pretty little rainbows weren't very big or very selective, but they sure were fun to hook, and they were obviously very hungry. Almost any dry fly pattern we'd try seemed to work wonders. It was the kind of fly-fishing that reminds me of wading a river in the western part of the lower 48; pretty flow, shallow riffles, and lots of little, hungry trout.

The Wulffs and Renegades I tied-on worked wonders – boosting my success ratio and also my confidence. Little by little I began to realize that my muscles were regaining some of their suppleness, and that I could still catch fish and might end up living, in spite of all the high water we'd faced that June.

I'd selected a 9 foot, 5-weight, graphite fly rod that morning, while Eli had chosen a 10-foot, 4-weight. Both rods seemed to be about right for the task at hand, although I questioned the need for using a 10-foot rod on that little stream. But, that's the way it is when you're fishing new water all the time; if I had fished that stream earlier I'd have selected either a 3-weight or a 4-weight instead of a 5, but since neither Eli nor I had ever *seen* that particular stream before, neither of us had any way of knowing what we were getting into.

To my way of thinking it was just another of the many situations where a 9-foot rod proved to be totally acceptable for the fishing at hand. Not too long, not too short. For a reel, I'd chosen one of my beloved Orvis CFO III's.

Eli was fishing his new, immaaculate and very lovely, Able TR-2 trout reel, a black jewel of a fly reel finished to perfection featuring exceedingly close tolerances.

Eli's an outstanding fly-fisherman, but he also has an excellent sense of humor. That's just one of the reasons I choose to fish with him whenever I can, and I've dubbed him *Eli* – a name that just sort of fits – because he's an individual with a very likeable, amiable, easy-going, johnny-come-lately personality.

It doesn't hurt that Eli has absolutely no understanding of how good he is, but, then again, maybe he's so good because he fishes more than any other living human. At least it *seems* that way.

Eli and I were both impressed with Greg Liu's professionalism and widespread knowledge as a fishing guide. Greg was always quick with a helping hand and he carried a pleasant, very professional attitude along with him. *He also carried a 12-gauge sawed-off shotgun –just in case* – another thing I've come to appreciate in fishing guides.

Whew! But that bear *stank.*

Obviously, this wasn't Greg Liu's first attempt at guiding. Later, when I asked him about it, I wasn't surprised to learn that he'd guided professionally for something like a dozen years, all toll. The previous couple of seasons he'd guided for another Alaska lodge, even serving one season guiding fly-fishers over in Russia, adding a little *crem de la crem* to his resume.

Like his tackle-dealing father, Alan Liu, Greg Liu has a comprehensive knowledge of the history of much of fly-fishing's finest rods and reels - everything from Garrisons and Gillums, to the technology of today's ultra modern graphites. His knowledge also extends to fly reels, everything from the Hardys, the Ballans, and the Peerless models to the most modern Able, Pate, and Charlton saltwater reels.

The following morning Bernie flew Eli, Logan, Greg Liu and me down to a wonderful char stream where we hooked char after char – all morning, til three in the afternoon, char in the four to five pound range – by swinging 24-foot, Teeny T-200 sinktip lines through those fairly swift, moderately deep currents.

Ironically, for some strange reason, Eli's favorite Alaska fly pattern- *the White Zonker* - was failing to catch many char that morning. We all knew the fish were there – *heck, we could see them flash out there in the riffles* – but still, after several passes, *few takers*. With it's luminous, metallic/pearl, mylar body and it's flowing, white rabbit wing, tied on a size-4, long shanked hook, the White Zonker probably officially qualifies as being a smolt pattern – although it readily passes as a 'flesh fly pattern' too. That particular morning was one of the few times Eli's favorite Alaska fly pattern just wasn't pulling 'em in.

So, recalling what had worked so well for John Gierach and me a couple of years earlier in those beautiful Tikchik streams, instinctively, I found myself reaching in my vest for my large zip-lok bag (my grab bag of rusty, old, many still wet, fairly ugly flies that I dislike, mostly, but am forced to go to every once in a while). Rummaging through the bag I eventually spied a size-4, Olive *Electric Woolly Bugger*, probably the very fly I'd fished with Mr. Gierach a couple of summers earlier. This pattern had worked wonders for me on char on several previous occasions – actually, on char, rainbows, *and* on steelhead.

Somehow, that morning, I just had *this feeling* that Olive would work again.

I didn't murmer a word of switching flies to Eli. On my first cast, halfway through the swing I felt that good, old, solid tug – the unmistakable, heavy 'take' of a char grabbing my fly, right at the turn.

Instantly my flyline tightened and I held on for dear life as a strong powerhouse of a char (about a 24-incher it turned out) applied the horsepower offering a deep, twisting battle. I was fishing one of my favorite graphite rods that day, a 10-foot, 5-weight, a rod that has proved to be exceptionally versatile and extremely long casting.

"Hey, Dan...What fly are you using?" Eli shouted across the stream.

Eventually I told him, and Eli switched flies and began catching char, too. The action soon became so intense that, finally, our guides, Logan and Greg, had to get in on the fishing.

Why not? Heck, we begged them to join us.

It didn't take Logan long to take the hint. He promptly waded out to the middle of the river to some big, swirling, deep riffles, where, sure enough, he promptly proceeded to hook into a couple of large, chunky rainbows (both big hens) that managed to drag him well down stream.

It dawned on me that Eli and I had been so completely satisfied with fishing for char after char that we'd totally overlooked the possibilities of any rainbows being present. It occurred to me once again how odd it can be at times, and how much a mental thing fly-fishing can be. I enjoy fishing for rainbows as much as anyone, yet, it hadn't even occurred to me to try for rainbows that morning. After all, we were out there fishing for char - *were we not?*

Hmmm. Food for later thought. And maybe evidence that char are more interesting than many anglers are led to believe.

Oh, well - neither Eli nor I were disappointed with either the fishing *or* our efforts. We'd both experienced what would go down into our memories as one of the finest mornings of wet fly-fishing we'd *ever* experienced.

Before we knew it, 3:00 rolled around and Bernie came flying in in his Beaver to pick us up for our return to Wood River Lodge.

Darned if I didn't go and leave my lucky blue and green Patagonia Fleece Jacket lying on that grassy hillside.

That morning's fishing had been an arctic char classic. Time had passed altogether too quickly. I would have *sworn* it was only one o'clock. But, that's how it is when you're having fun, when fly-fishing Alaska under ideal weather conditions.

Later that evening, after dinner, we'd fish the lovely Agulawok, me with a 5-weight bamboo rod, and Eli with a 9-foot, 4-weight. We'd fish until we'd had our fill of the premier dry fly rainbow fishing to be found out in front of the lodge.

A couple of days later, sitting in Dillingham Airport, waiting for our commercial flight to arrive and take us back to 'civilization,' Eli and I both had to pinch ourselves to realize that our fly-fishing trip of a lifetime had finally come to an end.

For me, after fishing at four of Alaska's best lodges – not to mention some of its ultimate rivers for nearly three straight weeks

– leaving was a quadruple blow. Outside, Papa John Ortman restarted his pretty, newly-painted red and white Cessna-185 on amphibs and began his flight back to the Tikchiks.

An hour later we landed at Anchorage International Airport. Eli's wife was there to meet us when we arrived.

Asked if i d like a ride home, I politely refused, declining on the grounds that my wife was on her way to pick me up. In reality, I just wanted a few more minutes to practice my speech. In a very short time, I realized, I'd begin the apology I'd practiced over and over in my mind for the past four days.

My plea would begin something like, "...Never, ever.. again will I take on so much responsibility and leave for so long, and, never, ever...never again will I spend nearly three weeks out fly-fishing...my dear."

Or something along those lines. I'd perfect it before I reached home, I figured. Whatever I'd end up saying, however, I knew it would be one of the most important presentations I'd ever make.

I waved goodbye to Eli and his wife, and hailed myself a cab.

Fifteen minutes later I could see that my prayers had been answered. My wife's car was still in the garage, so it appeared that she was still living at home. Nice, too, was that none of my fly rods or reels could be seen out in the street.

Fortunately my speech went all right, although I must admit I did feel *some* guilt for being the selfish fly-fishing compulsive I've become of late. Tomorrow I'd clean the garage, take out the garbage, and just to be a good sport, I'd wash both cars and clean up from the dachshunds around the yard.

Somehow, just then, I just didn't have the heart to tell my wife I'd be leaving on yet another fly-fishing assignment the following weekend. *That* explanation, I decided, would be better served over a fine Italian meal at any restaurant whatsoever of my wife's choosing.

Fly-Fishing Adventure #6

High Adventure Air's

Camp For A King

From *February/March '95 Issue*
Salmon Trout Steelheader magazine

"There she is... That's the river!" High Adventure Air's
pilot, Richard Ried, announced over the Piper Navajo's intercom.
"I'll circle around a little lower so you can all take a closer look!"

Easing back on the throttle, our pilot lowered the flaps –
turning the twin-engined Piper out across the tundra, and then
back again, crossing over a bend in the river. Below us, I glimpsed
a tiny outboard-powered motorboat as it made its way upstream
against the river's main current.

"Probably a native fisherman out trying to make a living" I
thought to myself as I strained to catch another glimpse of
Alaska's famed Nushagak River.

"Some of the best salmon fishing in Alaska is right below us,
but don't count out hooking into some trophy grayling and
rainbows, too," our pilot continued.

From the air it was easy to see that the 'Nush is a big, *wild*
river. There are few roads in this part of Alaska - save for a very

few, scattered here and there, most to be found nearer the larger native villages.

Our journey had begun only an hour and a half earlier but nearly 300 miles away at the town of Soldotna, Alaska, located near Kenai, where Greg, Mark, and Sandy Bell of High Adventure Air make their headquarters.

Earlier that morning my fishing partner, Tom Coomer, and I had driven down the Kenai Peninsula to Soldotna from our homes in Anchorage. While boarding the airplane we were introduced to four other anglers who we'd accompany on this Alaska fishing adventure - a trip primarily aimed at fishing Alaska's huge, 40 to 60 pound king salmon. Although Tom and I are essentially fly-fishermen by habit, both of us welcomed this opportunity to experience and fish the famed 'Nushagak drainage with High Adventure Air.

Lowering the flaps full, Richard gently set the Navajo down on a dirt landing strip overlooking the native village of New Stuyahok, a surprisingly modern fishing village built on the banks of the big Nush. Our trip from Soldotna had taken us directly over the very tallest peaks in the awesome Iliamna Mountain Range, and directly over huge Lake Iliamna, itself. Ironically, from an altitude of 11,500 feet North America's second largest fresh water lake had looked like but a very large pond on the tundra far below.

Presently we were met by a man who drove up on a 4-wheel drive ATV vehicle. He introduced himself as Joe Tweedy, High Adventure's head fishing guide in this region of Alaska. High Adventure operates varying fishing experiences throughout the southcentral and Bristol Bay regions, not to mention a complete array of fall hunting expeditions in Alaska.

We quickly learned that Joe was the man who'd be guiding us around the river for the next five days, taking us to some of the best salmon fishing in the entire state. It was easy to see that he was an extremely experienced fishing veteran, having guided on several of Alaska's finest rivers over the years. A few minutes later we were also introduced to Dean Stover, High Adventure's chief chef, who'd soon surprise us by creating truly gourmet cuisine in a very wilderness setting. Like Joe, Dean Stover was also an experienced Alaska river guide.

Naturally, our first task was to get our gear to where camp is located. This was accomplished by making a hour's jet-boat ride upstream - offering us a good chance to see the river *up close and personal,* experiencing the many sights and wildlife of that area. High Adventure had provided their guides with two large aluminum outboard riverboats - fully capable of handling all our belongings as well as the six of us anglers. The journey upriver proved to be exceptionally picturesque. Having a quality camera along is essential.

Before we knew it we arrived at High Adventure Air's deluxe King Camp - found at a pristine location selected on a naturally groomed corner of land, just where a small, clear-waterd stream enters the main river. There, we could see that the Nushagak River is a big, glassy, but very powerful, 200+ yard-wide flow. This year, the river was higher than normal, Joe had told us, much like many of the other rivers in the Bristol Bay region of Alaska were. Seems spring rains and a late season snowfall the previous winter had added a couple of feet more water to the drainages than was usual.

During our upstream journey we'd noticed that the native villages we'd passed (Nunachuak and up to Koliganek) showed that several kings - *large, bright kings* - had been netted, and in what appeared to be very good numbers. We could only surmise that this meant that ample amounts of additional kings must still be in the river.

During our next four days of fishing these assumptions proved to be correct.

Fishing Alaska's Nushagak River can best be described as being a wilderness fishing adventure. Usually there were few other fishermen to be seen during any one day at the Nushagak's best angling spots, and most of these fishermen were natives who seemed to have all the time in the world to enjoy catching their sportfish limits of dime bright pacific salmon. During a season all five species of salmon are available at the 'Nush - the only specie we wouldn't be taking during our stay was cohos, or silver salmon. Our visit to the 'Nush occurred at the end of June. Since we were making our visit in late June, the silvers' arrival was still a few weeks away, yet. High Adventure Air operates their wilderness fishing camp June 20th to July 25th annually.

One of the advantages we noticed right away about camp was that the river was always only a few steps away, always there, always flowing, always waiting to be fished. Unlike some lodges offer, after meals, guests can walk a few steps to the river and fish to their hearts' content. In mid-summer, with the sun not setting completely until something like two in the morning (and then only for a couple of hours) it never really gets dark in this region of Alaska. Consequently, during June and July of the year a serious fisherman can enjoy all the angling he can possibly muster.

Are there decent numbers of salmon and trout to be found at the 'Nush?

Better than decent. Much better.

There are amazing numbers of salmon to be caught in the Nushagak River. We were genuinely astonished at the numbers of migrating salmon we discovered, but with the high water, the trout were holding deep. Those that we hooked and released were profusely spotted, as pretty as any rainbows I've ever encountered. Later, after our trip, I learned that the escapement for king salmon, alone, in the Nushagak river numbered 95,900, with only an estimated 5000 kings being taken by sport fishermen in '94.

Peering into the river through good quality polarized sunglasses, a contuinuous stream of single-file salmon could be seen at nearly any given time - appearing as a never ending string of salmon venturing on a never-ending journey. We soon found that, while gazing through good, amber or brown-colored, polarized lenses a person can stand on the banks of the Nushagak and literally count the hundreds of salmon passing by as if the fish were part of a never ending procession:

Look! There's One,...two,...three, four....five, six, seven....eight....salmon. There's a king! There's a sockeye, followed by another king, there's a pink...there's a chum...and so on.

On and on the never-ending procession of migrating salmon continued. Salmon by the hundreds. Salmon by the thousands.

Without polarized lenses there would be only the constant glare of the river's surface.

For me, it was interesting for to note that the salmon's singular path was fairly close to the river's banks - possibly only thirteen or fifteen feet out and about that same distance deep. Taking off our polarized glasses the salmon's path was just slightly out of sight of the average human's vision.

After arriving at camp and enjoying a spot of lunch (Did I mention that the food at King Camp was great?) Joe and Dean invited us to join them for a bit of angling for some of their behemoth Alaskan kings. Donning our vests and grabbing our gear, it wasn't but a few minutes later that Joe led us downstream to a pretty, little, secluded spot on the river, a confluence near where another moderate flow enters in. There Joe rigged-up the casting gear for kings as I strung-up my flyrod in case of a grayling rise. The action for salmon didn't take long to begin.

Tom was one of the first of our party to hook-up that afternoon, and as usual, even though I've spent several years traveling to and fishing Alaska's premier rivers, I'm always surprised at the power a fresh-from-the-ocean king salmon can deliver - along with the amount of endurance it requires to handle one of these huge fish on a sport fishing rod. Soon after Tom's 30-pounder, a guest in the other boat whooped, setting the hook on what turned out to be a 45-pound chome-bright king - this one making Tom's fish appear only average - which it was. Tom's next king, a twenty-five pounder, was quickly released. While Tom was busy hauling-in behemoth fish, I fidgeted with my 4-weight fly rod, ready for grayling on dry flies.

Ocassionally an Alaska angler will hook a 'jumper' king.
Usually this equates to 30 pounds of airborne power. Jumpers
aren't common, really, and no, they don't jump anything like wild
rainbows do, but often hens, or female kings (and often jacks, or
immature males) will perform surprising antics at the end of a
fishing line. Tom hooked into a couple of these fish. I did my
best to get a picture - but, *alas!* No cigar. My timing was simply
wrong. Every time I'd put the camera away...

What about the river? How should it be rated? Well, as a
salmon stream, even under the high water conditions we faced that
June, I'd have to rate the Nushagak as a solid eight on the ten
scale. Granted, an individual would necessarily have to spend a
few weeks exploring the area to ascertain the very best spots for
finding resting schools of any particular species of salmon, to really
get to know the river well, but fortunately for us, High
Adventure's guides knew the river well enough. As guests, all we
had to do was sit back, relax, and battle big, powerful silver-dollar
kings and mint-bright sockeyes coming through.

"*Not bad duty*" I thought to myself. With the many
picturesque surroundings we had as backdrops - it certainly beat
city life with all it's stop lights and traffic - *that was for sure.*

Pass me another cold soda won't you?

Unquestionably, the best angler in our group proved to be a
lady. Hailing from southcentral Alaska, and living on the banks of
a large salmon river, this woman had become deadly with her very
unusual but highly effective self-taught fishing technique.

Apparently, by fishing salmon almost every day during the
summers, this woman had learned how to hook fish from the bank

using a fly rod like none of the rest of us had ever imagined of doing. One evening after a fine meal of T-Bone steaks and all the trimmings she even tried to teach Tom and me how she did it, but, unfortunately, although her advice seemed understandable and fairly logical *at the time*, I, for one, was beyond the point of really comprehending just what it was she was trying to teach us.

"How does she do it?" I turned and asked Tom.

"Darned if I know!" he answered.

I remember shaking my head, turning, stepping away, and talking to myself - *I remember saying something about how happy I was to be but a simple dry fly fisherman.*

For tackle, she used an unusual -to me, at least- equipment combination, although it obviously didn't seem strange to her *or* to the salmon after salmon she kept hooking. For a rod she employed an ultra-lightweight, very expensive, state-of-the-art, 9-foot, 8-weight fly rod. Her reel was a rather heavy, but very quality, polished brass saltwater model, a reel offering a stout drag.

Surprisingly, she didn't cast her offering out very far from where she stood on the river's bank. If anything, she showed us we were continually casting far too much line. Actually, she didn't cast it - she'd lob the fly, (sometimes underhanded) using a highly developed, but seemingly very unorthodox method of "plunking" her payload to her nearby target. Another unusual technique she employed was to use two to four 3/0 split shot *in conjunction* with a high-density sinking tip line: this technique got the goods down for her *-and fast-* right to where the fish were traveling.

Instead of using any type of 'strike indicator,' she'd simply allow her little 'pinkie' finger to feel the strikes for her. Those anglers who've fished Alaska's pacific salmon will know that sometimes - too often, in fact - a salmon's take *can seem* less than staggering. Often, an angler can barely feel a salmons' 'strike' when a fish 'nips at a fly.

What fly did she use? If I told you it was a merely a simple chartreuse and orange yarn fly tied to a size-1 Eagle Claw hook would you believe me?

True.

The fishing on this trip was everything I'd hoped it would be, but what I learned to appreciate most were the comforts to be found back at camp. Greg and Mark Bell of High Adventure had done a very creditable job of erecting a camp fit for a king. Hot water was available at any given time. Somebody want to take a shower? No problem - private facilities had been erected both for the taking of showers as well as for the latrine. The kitchen tent wss large and comfortable, and the food they served at King Camp rivaled several major lodges I've visited.

Looking back on the trip, everyone in camp had seemed to find what it was he or she had been seeking. Tom eventually hooked the 40-pound king salmon he'd been wanting, while I finally managed to land a couple of those heavily-spotted rainbows that make a fly-fisherman's adrenaline flow. One angler in camp put on a nightly display of battling all species of available salmon in front of camp - while another angler found the solitude and peace he'd desired by sitting back and enjoying that remote wilderness the calm, soothing sounds of the river, and the cool breezes twisting through the valley.

Our five days at High Adventure Air's King Camp proved to be a extraordinary wild river experience. It was exciting coming to know one of Alaska's ultimate rivers intimately. Over the past decade I've made it a hobby of experiencing and fly-fishing all I can of Alaska's best rivers, so, for me, adding the big 'Nush to my list was something that meant a lot.

Looking back, hooking into four different varieties of large, powerful salmon together with visiting those native villages we came across proved to be the stuff great memories are made of. Members of our party commented on how interesting it had been to meet and converse with the Alaskan natives we encountered. Each village was similar to the others with its row upon row of red, hanging salmon filets, drying in the sun - essential survival gear of the first order for those native families that exist in remote regions of Alaska.

Tom and I both appreciated the luxury we'd had of relying on experienced fishing guides to take us to the best fishing spots. We'd reveled in superb salmon fishing, relaxed in comfortable camp accomodations, and had enjoyed close camaraderie with the others in our group. And, yes, just to be sociable, Tom and I had both sampled generous helpings of Dean Stover's delicious streamside gourmet cuisine.

Several of the members of our party had commented on how affordable the trip was, being approximately only one-third the cost of a standard Alaska lodge fare. And, that includeded the twin-engined Navajo flight from and back to Soldotna, not to mention deHavilland Beaver shuttle flights to villages.

What more is there to a Alaska wilderness fishing experience?

On our final day, sure enough, just about the time I'd finally gained a good feel for the river and had developed a genuine appreciation for the Nushagak setting with all it's cliffs and varying terrains and all it's bald eagles and it's wildlife, pilot Richard Ried was down waiting for us at the end of our downstream float - down at *New Syuyahok* airstrip, only an hour's drift below camp.

Not wanting to leave, we thanked Joe and Dean for the experience they'd provided us with. Reluctantly we boarded the Navajo twin again, waiting to make the flight back to Soldotna again - back to reality - back to 'civilization' as they call it.

Civilization? I'll take a camp on the banks of the Nushagak River anytime.

We fastened our seatbelts as Richard adjusted the throttle and revved the engines. Suddenly the Navajo gained speed and lifted off. Joe and Dean were standing at the edge of the airstrip waiving goodbye.

A glance around the cabin told me that each of us had quietly said a personal farewell to a wilderness fishing adventure of a lifetime that had carved an indellible spot in our hearts.

Below us, the big 'Nush could be seen winding across the rolling tundra, continuing on its steady, seaward flow. Then, slowly, it disappeared under a layer of thin, scattered clouds. At 10,000 feet we came into warm, bright sunlight, as Richard trimmed the Navajo, cruising along at about 160 knots.

Suddenly I realized that yet another Alaska fishing adventure of a lifetime had come to an end. A glance at Tom showed he'd enjoyed his five days on the river, too. It was obvioius he didn't want to return to civilization any more than I did.

"They always end too quickly, don't they?" I muttered.

Alaska's wild rivers can do that to a person.

Through the twin's window I peered out upon a stark, clear, seemingly endless Alaska sky. I couldn't help but ask myself: *What had I enjoyed more?* The great fishing we'd had, or the remarkable wilderness adventure we'd experienced on that big, glassy, but very wild and uniquely remote river they call the Nushagak?

Then it occurred to me. A few years earlier I'd done a magazine story for High Adventure Air I'd entitled,

"Little River - Big Fish."

For describing this experience I'd consider calling it,

"Big River - Big Fish."

That title would certainly fit.

Anglers wishing to experience this wilderness Alaska fishing trip should contact:

Mark, Greg, or Sandy Bell
High Adventure Air
P.O. Box 486
Soldotna, Alaska 99669
Telephone: (907) 262-7333

Fly-Fishing Adventure #7

A Fly-Fishin' Mission
Iliamna and The Newhalen

"I think we should go for it" Andy said over the telephone. "Super Cub's all ready, and I've heard the reds are running *thick* over at the Newhalen right now. The weather looks good – my opinion is, I think we should get ourselves over there!"

I had to admit: Andy MacLeod was right. It *was* July 7, after all – the perfect time to fly-fish for Alaska's powerful incoming sockeyes (or red salmon) with a fly.

On the other hand, as my wife had only recently reminded me'd, I'd spent little time devoted to my job duties in Anchorage of late. Fortunately, however, my advertising clients seemed to be on 'summer cruise control.' Just maybe, I thought, *maybe I could* slip away for a few additional days without causing too many waves. Besides, I reasoned, it was summer in Alaska, the season I had waited many long, cold months for – and besides, Andy's logic concerning sockeyes and Iliamna *did* make for a very strong arguement. With any luck at all, advertising would still be there for me when I returned – just as I knew that the sockeyes and rainbows would wait for no one.

Besides, Eli was off fly-fishing for salmon somewhere – heaven only knew where – seemed nobody'd heard from him in days.

Best of all, as Andy had mentioned, the weather did appear perfect for flying (*bluebird weather* they call it) – very promising, indeed. It appeared to be a perfect time to venture over through Lake Clark Pass to the Iliamna country Andy and I both love.

Instinct being the better part of rationalization, Andy MacLeod and I were on our way fishing.

"Let's go for it, Andy!" I answered. "We're only young once. I'll meet you at your 'cub at Merrill Field Saturday morning!"

The weather stayed good. So good, in fact, that neither Andy or I had ever seen Lake Clark Pass as calm or as clear as it was the afternoon we flew from Anchorage. Lake Clark, itself, appeared as a giant, aqua blue, liquid mirror, appearing like an oil painting of an opal-blue dream, an ultra- picturesque lake reflecting a myriad of pristine, Alaska snow-capped mountains.

"Jay Hammond's sure got good taste in real estate" I said over the headset as we made our way toward Nondalton. Below, over to our left, flowed the ultra-clear, green-hued, beautiful Tazimina River that empties into Six-Mile Bay.

Below us, a cow moose and her calf greeted us from the middle of a shallow tundra pond. Visibility seemed endless. Not a cloud in the sky. Over to our right was the beginning of the Newhalen River, the large, blue-green drainage that connects Lake Clark with huge Lake Iliamna. Behind us, to our starboard was the township of Port Alsworth, a series of airstrips and watery coves, cabins, and a scattering of lodges.

By this time we'd been flying for nearly two and a half hours; a pretty ride, to be sure, but a fairly long time to be cooped-up in an airplane with a rear seat about the size of a grocery cart.

Following the flow of the Newhalen brought us directly to Iliamna. There, Andy circled once and then lowered the flaps, lining up on the long, dirt Iliamna airstrip. After a gentle landing Andy taxied off the runway, swinging the Cub around, where we parked outside Lem Batchelder's *Iliamna Airport Hotel*. While climbing out and unloading our gear I caught glimpse of Lem waving from the steps of his newly remodeled hotel.

Over the past couple of years Lem and his wife, Annesia, have done a formidable job of revamping the old building. Iliamna Airport Hotel has always offered valued respite from the wind, but now, good food, clean rooms, hot showers, warm beds, and generous portions of comfort are the order of the day. That might not sound like a lot at first, but trust me, in bush Alaska, generous portions of good food and comfort can go a long way. For the average salmon fisherman desiring a little respite from the wind and weather, or for those not wishing to spend three or four nights in a tent during sockeye season, Lem's Iliamna Airport Hotel provides an attractive alternative.

A quarter mile away, over at Iliamna Air Taxi – where commercial airliners arrive from Anchorage and offload – seemingly hundreds of travelers were either just arriving or leaving via ERA's daily, to and from Anchorage flights. The place was *busy* – literally swarming with salmon fishermen. In fact, I'd never seen Iliamna more crowded. But, there was good reason. After all, it *was* sockeye season in Alaska, and the Newhalen

River is one of the state's prime –easily accessible– sockeye fisheries.

Despite all the commotion, Tim and Nancy LaPorte seemed cool and as organized in assisting travelers. Somehow Tim and Nancy seem to manage to perform all the tiny miracles they do on a daily basis. Along with caribou hunting season a few weeks later, the sockeye salmon season is one of the busiest times of the year for the little airport town called, Iliamna, Alaska.

Andy and I had talked of flying down to the Kvichak River at the west end of Lake Iliamna just where it empties out of the lake, but our bladders needed a rest and Iliamna looked very good by the time we arrived. I'd wanted to introduce Andy to Brian Kraft, the new operator of nearby Big Mountain Lodge, but the winds were picking up, slightly, and the hamburgers at Lem's smelled too good for any more flying that day.

Suddenly, Dick Carnell, an assistant guide and pilot who works with Bob Cusack at Cusack's Alaska Lodge walked up. Dick, it seemed, had just arrived on the ERA flight from Anchorage.

'Why don't you and Andy join us for a couple of days over at the lodge at Kakhonak for a couple of days, Dan?" Dick asked. "After all, Bob and I won't be guiding any clients for two more days, yet. Why don't you guys come over and join us over at the Copper? Maybe you can teach Cusack how to fish!"

Before either Andy or I could answer Dick added, "Bob's probably waiting for us down at the lake by his airplane down right this minute – as soon as I can claim my baggage we'd better get down there – *pronto!*"

A glance over at Andy told me it was more than okay with him if we passed on fishing the Newhalen for a couple of days. The sockeyes would be in – thick – for the next couple of weeks, so that settled it: Andy and I were headed for Kakhonak for a couple of days with the infamous Bob Cusack and his sidekick, Mr. Richard Carnell.

Sure enough, Bob was waiting down at the lake by his Cessna 185, just like Dick had said he'd be. It had taken us a half hour to retrieve Dick's bags and get over to where Bob was waiting from Iliamna Airport, but thanks to *Jimmy's Iliamna Taxi,* we finally arrived.

"Don't you guys ever work?" Bob teased uas we shook hands. Quickly, we began loading our gear and fly rods.

"Mr. Cusack, Kind Sir," I said, "I'll have you know that, *as residents of the fine state of Alaska* we work our hands to the bone for eight months of the year– *all winter long!"* I added. "During summer," I continued, "whenever we can, anyway, we *fly*-fish - and we do this as often as we possibly can!" I emphasised.

"I think I get the picture" Bob gestured, holding up a finger.

"Okay...Get in the airplane - let's go fishin!"

Presently we were airborne, headed for Kakhonak on the 18-or-so minute flight it requires to cross Iliamna over to Pope/Vannoy country.

"How's Tony Sarp doing down at *Katmai Lodge* over on the Branch?" Bob asked over the airplane's roar. "How was the rainbow fishing over that way?" Bob continued.

"That Alagnak is one awesome river, as you well know, Bob" I replied. "I was able to manage several rainbows in the 23 to 24-inch range, but nothing huge this last trip. Maybe I'll do better in September if I can get back out there."

"Right now, the sockeyes are coming in *thick* over here - *extremely* thick this year, it fact." Bob emphasised. "Looks like more reds this year than for several previous years" he continued. "Greg Hamm over at Bear Foot Adventures is busy finishing-up with the final touches on his lodge and it's looking real nice. Look's like he'll be ready to bring in guests and guide clients over on the Copper next season."

That was a thing I had learned to appreciate about Bob Cusack. Whereas some lodge owners absolutely refuse to speak or associate with competitors, Bob Cusack always seems to go out of his way to assist those he can. Apparently, Bob Cusack feels secure enough within his personal abilities and with his personal clientele list that he doesn't need to waste much time playing petty politics games. In other words, Bob Cusack's an experienced pro - a master guide who seems to have an unusually good idea of what an Alaska experience should be, and what an Alaska lodge experience should deliver.

The weather continued to hold bluebird perfect - a bit unusual for Lake Iliamna country, really. The sky was absolutely clear, and visibility across the lake seemed endless. From my seat in Bob's Cessna I observed the myriad of tiny islands below us as seagulls circled beneath us.

"You know, Bob," I turned and said, "on days like this I believe I enjoy the flying almost as much as I do the fly-fishing, itself." I said.

"It's nice on pretty days like this" Bob quipped, "but, as you know," "it can be wicked out here at times when the wind's blowing" he added, casting a serious look in my direction. "It can be a real xxxxx at times!" Bob is seldom at a loss for words.

A minute later Bob cut the throttle, jacked down the flaps, and slipped the floatplane down through a green tundra valley, skimming over a panoramic little bay.

"Just take a look at those reds down there, boys!" Bob shouted, pulling the Cessna up for a second glance, as all eyes peeled down at the bay directly below us. The bay's banks were literally stacked with thousands upon thousands of sockeyes, or red salmon. The fish were in so thick they appeared black.

"*Reds Indeed!*" *Dick Carnell said.* "And by the hundreds of thousands!" So many fish that an ntrained eye might have thought the dark areas to be but mere rock structures.

Then Bob powered the Cessna up again, throttling up a touch, gaining a bit more altitude from which we could view the surrounding bays. Then he swooped us down again in preparation for a gentle water landing between a set of islands - protected and sheltered in a small, secluded bay. Finally, *Bob Cusack's Alaska Lodge* became visible. Located in a very picturesque setting, and highly secluded, Bob's lodge is built on top a small, rolling hilltop, almost hidden in the corner of a very private and very attractive bay.

"Did I tell you about my new, 33-foot aluminum boat I purchased the other day?" Bob asked us as he taxied the floatplane toward the lodge. "Actually, it was Dicky Boy, here, along with Greg Hamm over at Bear Foot Adventures who were nice enough to drive it across Lake Iliamna for me!"

You mean they actually motored across Lake Iliamna? I asked in disbelief.

"She only cruises at about 6 knots or so, but she's extremely seaworthy" Dick Carnell responded. "With those twin 115's she's got all the power in the world. We'll have to show 'er to you guys in a few minutess, after we unload our gear.

"I haven't named her yet, but she'll be just perfect for resting and feeding clients after a half-day's fishing, or before going back out for the afternoon and evening." Bob added.

With that Bob slid the airplane into the dock at his lodge. Andy and I helped unload our gear and rods from behind the rear seat of the floatplane. Andy and I were shown to the lodge and to our private rooms.

After a typical Cusack gourmet lunch consisting of pasta, fresh strawberries, tossed salad, and several slices of tasty homebaked bread and jams and jellies, Andy and I grabbed our fly rods and vests and followed Bob and Dick down, around the path, following a short trail that leads to the other side of the bay.

Five minutes later we arrived at the small inlet where Bob keeps his new boat. A first glance told me the boat was much larger than I had imagined it to be.

"*There she blows, boys!*" Bob exclaimed, pointing to his shiny, new, aluminum vessel. "Meet our new baby!"

Paul D. "Eli" Rotkis, with 47lb. halibut taken on a fly while fishing with Capt. Jimmy Seas of, *The Charter Connection,* out of Seward, Alaska. Eli hooked this fish in 130 feet of water using a G. Loomis, 12-weight GL3 fly rod, a Billy Pate 'Tarpon' fly reel, and a Scientific Anglers, 850 grain, sinking shooting taper. Fly was a 2/0 'White Zonker.'

The author examines his first 'Rockfish,' or Black Sea Bass caught on a fly. Located along cliffs and rocky outcroppings at saltwater's edge, such areas are frequently home to large numbers of this interesting saltwater specie. Sea Bass are readily attracted to disturbances at the surface and strike flies with reckless abandon. *The Charter Connection,* which operates out of Seward, knows many good places for hooking these sea bass.

Tony Weaver with 30lb. lingcod hooked while fishing with Jimmy Seas of *The Charter Connection,* Seward. Tony used a G. Loomis, 10-weight Mega fly rod, a Mackenzie 500 grain shooting taper line, and a big, bug-eyed leech pattern to attract this near-record fish. *Tony Weaver photo*

Seven, 4-unit-each 'condos' (28-total) make up unique, *Iliamna Lake Resort* located on North Shore of Iliamna. Each unit offers a modern kitchen and private, upstairs and downstairs bath. Each unit has two bedrooms.

It is early May and the snow on the ground has barely melted, and Paul D. "Eli" Rotkis is leading the author to one of his 'secret' Alaska lakes for a day of float tube fly-fishing. Eli made me swear I'd never divulge this lake's location to anyone – an easy task, since we went fishless this day, anyway.

Bob Trout of Alaska TROUTFITTERS located in Cooper Landing, Alaska, displays one of the monster rainbow trout he is famous for. Bob and Curt Trout have been guiding on the Kenai River for several seasons, and know the best areas for hooking trophy rainbows and Dolly Varden.

The author with a nice, 5-pound rainbow taken late one evening on the Newhalen River, at Iliamna, using a 40 year old, Nat Uslan, 5-strip, 5-weight bamboo fly rod. Fly was a size-4 'Jimmy's Smolt' pattern, tied by Jimmy Winchester, *ILR.*

This big, 28 1/2" 9-pound Alagnak rainbow was caught and released by Bill Herzog (editor, STS magazine) on a graphite, 5-weight fly rod while fishing out of *Tony Sarp's Katmai Lodge* in June of the year. Note the profuse spots on this lovely hen and the large, gaudy sculpin pattern Bill used.

The author talks with Craig Ketchum, owner of *Ketchum Air Service* in Anchorage, prior to flight from Lake Hood to TalStar Lodge located on Alaska's famed Talachulitna River. Ketchum's specializes in flying fishermen to remote locations, and operates several deHavilland Beavers and Otters (standard and turbo).

John Staser of Anchorage displays one of forty rainbow trout he caught and released in four hours while fishing out of Katmailand's, Kulik Lodge with author. Rainbows averaged between 16 and 23 inches – trip was during early August.

Curt Trout with magnificent Kenai River trophy rainbow hen, caught and released in late September. Curt and Bob Trout own and operate, "Alaska TROUTFITTERS," a guiding, raft, and drift boat rental business located in Cooper Landing, Alaska.

Polly Kansagrad displays large, 30" steelhead trout caught and released using G. Loomis 10-ft, 6-weight GLX fly rod. Fish was taken at Deep Creek in southcentral Alaska in late September.

Andy MacLeod with typical, sockeye (or red) salmon taken on fly at Iliamna's Newhalen River during early July. Fish was hooked in swift currents on 8-weight fly rod, fishing a Mackenzie, 25-foot, 300 grain sinktip, or shooting head line.

Bob Cusack, of *Bob Cusack's Alaska Lodge.* Bob is a master guide who has guided fishermen and hunters all over the state of Alaska. As you can see, Bob operates a fleet of floatplanes from his lodge located in Kakhonak, on the south side of Iliamna.

Nanci Morris, head guide at *Quinnat Landing Hotel,* in King Salmon with a fabulous, 14-pound Naknek River rainbow 'buck' taken on a size-2, weighted black leech pattern. Taken in late September, using a Teeny 'Mini Tip' fly line, from a new, state-of-the-art, G. Loomis, 4-piece, 8-weight GLX fly rod.

Tom Coomer displaying 5 1/2-pound, 24-inch Talachulitna
River rainbow trout taken during early August while fishing a
G. Loomis, 10-foot, 5-weight IMX fly rod. Caught and released
on a Ginger 'Bunny Bug,' or 'Flesh Fly,' fished from a 13-foot,
sinktip line. Talachulitna 'bows feature striking red fins.

The author with large, 11-pound Arctic Char taken at 'Ugashik Narrows' located on Alaska Peninsula while fishing out of *Quinnat Landing Hotel* in King Salmon with Dr. 'Joe' Chandler and Larry Smith. Rod was G. Loomis, 9 1/2-foot, 6-weight IMX. Ugashik Narrows is best known for its trophy grayling.

Kulik Lodge is situated between Kulik (upper) Lake and Nonvianuk Lake in Katmai, Alaska. Kulik is one of three lodges (Grosvenor and Brooks are the others) Katmailand offers to fishermen. These famed lodges have operated since 1950.

Kulik's main lodge building and dining hall. This immaculate, first class Alaska fishing lodge has built a reputation over the years featuring outstanding fishing, premier fly-outs, superb food and service, and comfortable, private guest cabins.

Alagnak River, 15-inch "small rainbow" taken on a size-14 Elk Hair Caddis during a grayling rise below an island in the 'Braids,' while fishing out of *Tony Sarp's Katmai Lodge.*

This phenomenal, 11-pound rainbow trout graces the cover of this book but deserves a full spread. Caught and released by Tony Sarp at Katmai Lodge on the Alagnak during late September on a 7 1/2-foot, G. Loomis, 3-weight, IMX fly rod using size-14 caddis dry fly. Photo courtesy of Trey Combs.

TalStar Lodge located on the famed Talachulitna River. Built amongst thick, lush ferns, TalStar features fishing right outside their door for five species of pacific salmon, rainbows, Dollies, and grayling, in season. Check with owners for best time of year for specie / species you desire. Good dry fly fishing in Sept.

Beautiful, heavily-spotted rainbow trout caught and released by author at Talachulitna River fishing out of TalStar Lodge. Flesh Patterns and Zonkers fished on sinktip lines were effective during our stay in early August. Photo taken by Tom Coomer.

Tom Coomer of Anchorage 'nymphing' a single-egg pattern on the lovely Tal, or Talachulitna River. Like Brooks, the Tal is one of those rivers that looks as if it was created primarily with fly-fishers in mind. Fortunately for its rainbow population (and its fly-fishers) the Talachulitna is a total catch and release fishery.

One of the delights of traveling to Alaska's premier fly-fishing locations is meeting some of Alaska's native peoples. These kids from the small town of Newhalen, near Iliamna, assisted me with my fly rods while I pulled on my neoprene waders.

Ketchum Air Service turbine Beaver, one of only sixty, or so, originally manufactured at the factory. Located at Lake Hood in Anchorage, Ketchum's operates five standard Beavers, three Cessna 206's, the turbine Beaver pictured, and a turbine Otter.

One of the modern, clean guest cabins at *TalStar Lodge*, located on the famed Talachulitna River. Situated very near the river, guests can enjoy meals and easily return to the river for fishing. Five species of pacific salmon are available (in season) along with rainbows, char, and arctic grayling.

John Ortman, Jr., of *Wood River Lodge* casting from a driftboat to one of the many rising rainbows in front of the lodge one evening after dinner. Grayling, Arctic char, and various salmon species are also available for the fly-fisher on the Agulawok.

Wood River Lodge as it appears from the lovely Agulawok River. Located in the Wood River / Tikchik Lakes region of western Alaska, this area is home to some of the finest 'mixed bag' fly-fishing available. Rainbows, char, grayling, salmon... how about maybe going for northern pike?... what will it be today?

Nanci Morris with another huge Alaska rainbow trout, taken at the Naknek River, just below Naknek Lake – near Brooks. As an Alaska fly-fishing guide, Nanci makes a habit of hooking and releasing these monsters on a regular basis.

One of a dozen, or so, private guest cabins located at Katmailand's premier Kulik Lodge. Each cabin includes a private shower and toilet. The main lodge is located only a few steps distant. Kulik Lodge has been a top fly-fishing destination for anglers from around the world since 1950.

If the author appears happy in this photo it's because he is. Twenty minutes after arriving at the lodge he and his guide grabbed their fly rods and motored up the Alagnak to the *Braids.* This 6-pound rainbow was hooked on the second cast. *Tony Sarp's Katmai Lodge,* photo by Ray Johnson.

Tony Weaver shown demonstrating a casting clinic during a video taping at *Bob Cusack's Alaska Lodge* on the Copper River in Iliamna. Rob Hood managed the microphone while Roger Miller worked the video camera.

Float tubing is almost as popular in Alaska (a state with 3,000,000 lakes) as it is anywhere. Here, a fly-fisher enjoys an afternoon's paddling for grayling and 'bows on one of several lakes within an hour's drive of Anchorage.

One of the main lodge buildings at *Tony Sarp's Katmai Lodge* on the Alagnak. The flight from King Salmon is about 18 minutes, taking the visitor over some scenic country. Katmai Lodge is constructed right on the banks of the Alagnak (or Branch) consisting of something like twenty buildings in all. Guests can arrive via either float-equipped or wheeled aircraft.

Piper Super Cubs are the undisputed kings at getting fly-fishers into remote lakes and rivers. 'Cubs can land and take-off in places other airplanes wouldn't even attempt. Here, Andy Macleod readies his 'Cub for a flight to Iliamna.

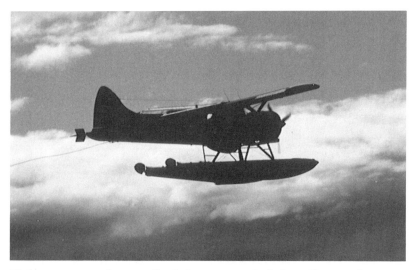

Today, more and more fly-fishers are scheduling fly-out day-trips and overnight trips to Forest Service cabins located throughout southcentral. Here, one of High Adventure Air's (Soldotna) deHavilland Beavers makes its way to Lake Clark country.

Jodi Andres with another large Kenai River rainbow taken by 'nymphing' a small, single-egg pattern using a strike indicator and a floating line. Jodi is only one of more and more women getting involved in the sport of fly-fishing.

Anglers used to fishing large rivers from foot will cover much more water when by drifting as shown here. Alaska TROUTFITTERS, in Cooper Landing, leases rafts or drift boats, along with offering half-day or full-day guide service.

Tom Coomer prepares his cataraft, 'The Kenai Kadillac,' for it's maiden voyage from Sportsman's Landing down to Jim's Landing. The upper Kenai River offers fly-fishers a good opportunity of hooking trophy rainbows and char mid-June thru mid-October.

Bob Cusack's Alaska Lodge. Built on a picturesque hill overlooking a panoramic bay, Bob Cusack's Alaska Lodge can handle up to 8 or 10 guests. Fly-fishing on the nearby Copper, and other fine Iiamna and Katmai rivers and streams. Bob Cusack is a master guide with years of Alaska experience.

Here is a front view of *Bob Cusack's Alaska Lodge* – taken from Kakhonak Bay. Cusack's guests are flown to several of the area's premier rivers for ultimate Alaska fishing experiences. Cusack's Lodge currently maintains a Cessna 182, a Cessna 185, a Cessna 206, and a Piper Super Cub, all on floats.

Ending a great day's fishing with a great meal is an integral part of any Alaska fishing lodge experience. All of the lodges mentioned in this book offer outstanding food. This gourmet meal was served at *Bob Cusack's Alaska Lodge* at Iliamna.

Grosevnor Lodge Manager, Dave Saurman, with fine Dolly Varden char taken at one of the rivers in Grosvenor Lodge area. Fish was caught and released using a 6-weight fly rod on a tiny, peach-colored egg-imitation fly, called an "Iliamna Pinkie."

Tony Sarp sharing a laugh with a couple of happy fly-fishers.

Dr. Leon 'Joe' Chandler of *Quinnat Landing Hotel* with a large (but small for Ugashik) Arctic Grayling caught and released in September of the year. Ugashik is classic grayling dry fly water, a spot reknowned over the years for its large grayling and great char fishing. Today, Ugashik is a strict catch and release only fishery.

During winter, many fly-fishers escape to warmer climates. Here, the author's companion, Alaskan Paul D. "Eli" Rotkis, displays one of several, large Yucatan Peninsula Bonefish caught and released while fishing saltwater flats.

"Yes, 33-feet of very seaworthy aluminum!" Carnell added.

"You ought to know, Dickey, 'ol boy!" Bob quipped. "You were the one who was crazy enough to drive her across Lake Iliamna!" Bob teased in typical Cusack fashion.

"*The Kakhonak Lady!*" I ventured. "*That's what you should name 'er,* I said aloud.

"Yeah, "*The Kakhonak Lady!*" Dick Carnell agreed.

In another minute or so the twin Evinrudes were warmed up and 'the screws' began to turn. Dick manned his familiar post at the helm and backed the boat out into open water as Bob scrambled up topside, on the lookout for rocks or possible obstacles in the area. Meanwhile, Andy and I began stringing-up our salmon rods. There was little question which specie of fish we were going out after this day: red salmon, or *sockeyes.*

By this time the rays of a warm July sun had begun to warm the aluminum vessel. A voice said, "Hey, Guys!" and we turned, and suddenly, there was my old friend, Bruce Johnson, Manager of nearby *Talarik Creek Lodge,* also a close friend of Bob Cusack's. Bruce and an assistant guide had been over fishing in that area and a minute later we watched them board a Cessna 206 and take off.

"I wouldn't be surprised if next year by this time Bob's new ship has a finished bathroom, a kitchen, bedrooms, a dining room, picnic tables with a view, and shower and maybe even a sauna," I said to Andy. After all, with several years of guiding clients on the Alagnak, working out of a houseboat (looking much like an old riverboat vaguely resembling those used in the old west) *who* in Alaska could know more about floating comfort than Bob Cusack?

Dick motored us across the bay to a point literally stacked with resting reds. The water just off the beach was nearly black from the thick concentrations of milling salmon all around us.

It occurred to me that later, possibly that next winter, I'd consider doing a story about this day spent with Bob Cusack and Dick Carnell and Andy. I thought about entitling it, *"Sockeyes in the Surf."*

Andy began hooking into reds immediately. Within a few minutes he was busy hauling-in scrapping sockeyes. One after another, Andy hooked and battled those powerful salmon on his 8-weight fly rod.

There's a certain technique required in getting *milling* sockeyes to take a fly - just as there's a certain technique required to get *migrating* sockeyes to strike. You'd think the two might be nearly identical, but both techniques are actually very different. I've got the migrating technique down fairly pat - but when it comes to milling fish, Andy MacLeod has the skills it takes to take salmon. And, no, I'm not talking about snagging fish.

What technique to use depends upon the depth of the water where the salmon are milling about. Use too fast of a sinking tip line and you'll whiz your fly right by the zone the fly needs to be at to effect good hookups. Conversely, use too light a line and your strip-ins will glide right over the salmon. I'd strung up a 9-weight fly rod using a 400-grain, 24-foot shooting taper, while Andy's MacKenzie, 25-foot 300 grain sinktip was doing a superb job. I

116

could tell by the first instant I made a cast that my 400 grainer was simply sinking right past all the fish – right to the bay's floor.

But the day was so pretty, and that warm, Alaska sunshine so welcomed that neither Bob nor I seemed to care much just then to take the time to switch lines. What became obvious was thefact that neither of us were that anxious to catch salmon just then. Bob and I were more than content just spending an afternoon in that warm Alaska sunshine, enjoying a day without clients or business cares, a beautiful day spent out in the wilds of Alaska, a day spent simply enjoying the experience of being alive and swapping lies in the panorama of The Great Land.

It was an afternoon spent talking about many of the characters we know in common in the 49th state. Visitors might have a difficult time understanding, but sometimes it's nice *just being there* , just going through the motions, not really pursuing a quary, simply enjoying the day and admiring the scenery. Bob and I must have spent an hour and a half just standing there chatting on that beach, spinning yarns and laughing about this Alaska character or that. Did you hear about what ol' Charlie did that night over at...

All the while Andy and Dick were busy out there hooking and fighting fish –busy hauling-in those potent sockeyes. As a trout enthusiast committed to catch and release it was easy for me to rationalize: no fish this afternoon? No problem. Anyway I looked at it, it sure beat working back in the city. Besides, I'd received all the enjoyment I'd come for just spending an afternnon with a colorful character named Bob Cusack.

Consequently, I decided to abandon any possible future story entitled, *"Sockeyes in the Surf."* Instead, I considered doing an article entitled, *"Farewell 'Civilized' World."*

On the next day Bob wanted to get Andy and me into some of that area's prime trout fishing. so after another delicious Cusack breakfast, Andy and I grabbed our gear and joined Bob in his 185, and were soon on our way to a pretty little trout stream located only a half hour or so from the lodge.

There, Bob dropped us off, promising to return at 3:00 pm; more than sufficient time for the two of us to fish to our hearts' content. Other clients, we'd learned, had fished this stream earlier that season, picking-up many small to medium rainbows, together with a several grayling – most fish taken at the surface on dries.

I had a 2-piece graphite 9-foot, G. Loomis 5-weight fly rod along with me that day, a rod I'd had custom made for me back in Anchorage at Custom Rods and Tackle. The rod's a beauty, utilizing a nickle silver and teak sliding band reel seat, and it is one of four or five rods I rely on regularly. Hal Thompson put the thing together for me using new, first-quality G. Loomis blanks. That 5-weight has proved to be a very versatile little tool; with pretty, rust-colored wraps over charcoal colored graphite.

For a reel I'd brought along my pair of silver, Orvis Anniversay CFO III's. Like I've mentioned, I always try to carry two identical reels just in case one gets damaged in any way.

For lines I could choose between either a Wulff Triangle Taper 4/5 floater on one spool, or a 5/6 Wulff floater on the other. That minor difference in line weight can make all the difference in the world between proper loading – especially when the wind is blowing.

The Wulff Triangle Tapers are easily among finest casting, best all around floating lines I've ever tried in Alaska, even though the Cortland 444SL and Scientific Mastery series lines are excellent, too. In my opinion, now that Wulff is making their fly lines in flame color (besides white) they're even better yet.

For starters, I decided to tie on a *Royal Wulff* as a searcher fly, just to see what it would do. Two drifts later I had my first fish of the afternoon, a chunky, 14-inch Grayling, its beautiful dotted and purpled dorsal fin flowing so gracefully above it as I reached down to hand it. Going with my instincts, I switched flies to possibly my favorite dry fly –a *Renegade*– and promptly proceeded to hook a small rainbow.

Since Andy and I had this place entirely to ourselves, and since this particular stream was fairly narrow, I decided it wouldn't be entirely comfortable competing with Andy, working my way down the stream the rest of the afternoon. Maybe I'd let Andy fish hisway downstream while I'd stayed at the top and fooled around near the outlet of the small lake. It occurred to me this would be the perfect opportunity to try a series of dry fly experiments.

Several times over the years I'd wondered: *What* differences could a fly-fisherman notice if he was to employ the efforts of five or six of the most popular dry flies in an area if that area was large enough so that the angler didn't "spook" all the fish around him? In other words, *Which* fly/s would produce the best results of the top five or six patterns tried?

A glance downstream showed me that Andy was slowly working his way down through the various holes. It occurred to me I'd probably never have a better opportunity to conduct such a dry fly 'test.' Since we had the spot all to ourselves and there were no other anglers around us, I decided to try the 'experiment,' to see if it would teach me anything.

Since my fly rod was already rigged up with a 5/6 Wulff Triangle Taper floating line, I decided to stay right where I was and continue fishing, standing exactly where I had been in the currents. I decided I wouldn't move and muddy the water around me. I was fishing a knotless, tapered, 9-foot, Scientific Anglers leader that day, tapered down to 3x – with a couple of additional feet of 4x Orvis Super Strong leader material knotted on via a double surgeon's knot. The end result was a leader of about eleven feet.

To be as fair as possible with each pattern I tried, I thought I'd attempt to repeat the exact, same process of greasing the fly, along with greasing the entire tapered leader with *green label*, or silicone-treated Mucilin. I'm a firm believer in leaders continually dragging dry flies down with them to their watery grave, so I often devote a little more time to rigging my dry fly systems than one might normally consider doing. To me it just makes sense to eliminate as much of the sinking potential as possible by greasing the entire leader along with the fly. I've tried most of the different types of fancy powders and fancy new sprays to keep flies floating, but if I had to choose just one method, I think, still I'd probably end up going with good, ol' green labled Mucilin. The secret to this process is applying the grease BEFORE the fly has become wet – at all.

I gave a yellow Humpy several casts, allowing it to drift along the water's surface just like the others, but after all was said and done it simply didn't deliver the same performance or results as either the *Royal Wulff* or the *Renegade* had done. Was this because I was starting to "spook" the fish in the area around me? Were less fish coming to the fly because I'd spooked 'em? Or were the poor results because the fish simply didn't like the looks *-or the size-* of the new fly? Was it a question of "matching the hatch" or simply that the fish didn't like the looks of the Humpy?

That's about the time it occurred to me: My first two flies had employed one thing in common:

Peacock herl bodies.

I had to admit; peacock herl, with its iridescent, seemingly magical way of attracting fish had frequently produced fine results for me over the years. The Griffiths' Gnat –another favorite of mine – ehibits peacock, too. Peacock simply seems to impart an inherent, life-like, 'buggy' look to a fly that frequently causes near immediate results. What would happen now if I were to untie the Humpy and try one of the Peacock patterns again? I wondered.

I soon found myself reaching in my fly box for a size-14 or size-12 *Griffith's Gnat,* just to see. Over the years I've found the services of this fly to be better than excellent - particularly for arctic grayling. The times I've used it (several) the grayling and rainbows have seemed to be quickly attracted. Often they'd rise almost immediately and would quickly inhale a *Griffith's* like a kid reaching out for candy. I wondered what would happen now?

I found I had but a couple of old, fairly used-looking, size-14 Griffith's patterns with me this day. Nevertheless, I'd tied one on and greased it – just like the others. On my second cast, almost as quickly as it fluttered to the surface (employing a parachute delivery) a 14-inch rainbow rose and quickly tucked the fly neatly in the corner of it's mouth. Instantly turning back down, the fish tried to escape with it's easy meal.

Ah Ha~!! Peacock, I've rediscovered you! I thought to myself as I played the small rainbow to hand. I had to admit; I felt much excitement at such an immediate response. Releasing that rainbow unharmed, I quickly false cast the Gnat several times over my head to redry the fly.

It occurred to me for the thousandth time how thrilling it is to hook rainbows and grayling at the surface using a dry fly. There's just something so natural about it - something so refreshing about fishing the surface with a floating fly. For me, it ranks right up there with most other types of fly-fishing – both fresh and saltwater – that I've experienced.

To me it's ironic, how, many hundreds of anglers venture to Alaska each year just to have a chance at hooking into a king salmon weighing something from 25-70 pounds. I've often wondered how absurd it would sound to these anglers if they knew I'd rather catch one 14-inch rainbow trout on a dry fly than to hook into one of those behemoth kings – either on a fly, *or* on gear. To each his own as they say.

Suddenly an hour and a half had crept by and I could see Andy working his way back up through the bushes toward me. Cranking in my flyline I clipped the fly on the keeper and worked my way over through the currents and climbed up the hillside where I met him.

Andy's first words were: "I hope you've had as much fun with these small trout as I have this afternoon. I've had several fish on, especially down there at that one hole just around that bend down there" he said, pointing. Then he added, "I must have had eight or nine fish on down at that far hole. I'd forgotten what fun dry fly fishing for trout can be." he added.

I was pleased that Andy had really enjoyed himself. During the week, Andy's a very successful, hard working, dedicated businessman in the city. It was good to hear him sound like a school kid once again - now a grown kid who'd suddenly rediscovered what a wonderful sport fly-fishing for rainbows can be.

The wind was fairly howling in another half hour by the time 3:00 rolled around. Straining to listen, Andy and I soon heard Bob Cusack's Cessna-185 approaching from off in the distance right on schedule.

Considering those winds that afternoon, Bob Cusack would have to make what Andy and I both considered to be a very hairy landing on those choppy, 2+ foot waves that had suddenly sprung-up on the lake. Alaska's weather can be like that; one minute everything seems okay, then the next thing you know all hell can break loose. Whenever considering Alaska's weather there's usually one thing a fisherman can count on - *anything* and everything can happen in a day's time - and given half a chance it probably will.

Andy and I both realized that Bob's flying that afternoon would require the touch of a very expert bush pilot. "I wouldn't even attempt a landing in these winds" Andy muttered as we watched Bob fly over.

Andy was right. To succesfully land a floatplane in those winds would require simple, raw experience. Like Andy, had I been a pilot I don't think I'd have attempted to drop in for a visit in those gusts that particular afternoon. Fortunately for us, however, Bob Cusack hadn't wanted us spending the night out in that gathering storm. Later, when we asked him about the winds, Bob remarked he'd landed in weather 'far worse on several occasions.' Bob Cusack is, afterall, an Alaska master big game guide just as much as a fishing guide – and every body knows that bear guiding in Alaska means *expert* flying.

It was about then that I was reminded of Bob's comment earlier when I'd asked him about his years as a guide. His response was that he'd acquired over 10,000 hours of bush flying in Alaska's extremely wide variety of weather conditions!

10,000 hours? In single-engine bushplanes? Whew!

Back at the lodge Andy and I related the joys of our fishing to Bob and Dick as we sipped cold sodas. Bob and Dick had spent their afternoon doing chores around the lodge until the winds had come up and Bob had scurried over to fetch us.

Our stay at Cusack's had slipped by quickly. Now, suddenly, it was time to move out of the way for incoming clients and to hop over to the other side of the lake and begin our quest for sockeyes at the Newhalen. Neither of us could thank Bob or Dick enough for the hospitality they'd extended, and I found myself once again reminded of the fact that, even though we fly-fishers frequently find ourselves believing we're venturing out to the wilds of Alaska to experience the fishing – often, in reality, it's the people we come to know along the way that end up being the main attraction. Andy and I would remember our visit to Bob Cusack's Alaska Lodge for a long time.

Later that evening, across the lake over at Iliamna, Andy and I would resume our original plan to fly-fish the Newhalen River for sockeyes. It was about then that Andy told me that his wife had sent him on a mission to catch red salmon for the freezer for the coming winter. Apparently, the order had been something like, *"Don't come back without plenty of reds for the freezer."*

I liked that. I thought to myself, what a wonderful thing it would be to have a wife who demanded you go fishing.

I thought about how ironical fishermen's missions can be.

My own fishin' mission has always been to venture forth, to experience, to attempt to gather data (catch fish), attempt to photograph, and then attempt to share this information with others. Makes perfect logic and sense as far as I'm concerned. That way I can rationalize spending weeks away from all sorts of normal responsibilities - job, taking out the garbage, washing cars, etc. – all in the name of *gathering* information.

But Andy's mission put an entirely new twist on the subject. I had to admit: I liked it a lot. It had merit. To me it represented an entirely new slant on a fisherman's theory of relativity – one that I'd never even considered before. I could only imagine myself (keeping a straight face) saying to my own wife:

"...I'm off on a mission to catch 14-pound rainbows or I can't return to advertising!"

It reminded me of a line – uttered over and over in the movie, "The Blues Brothers. "

We're on a mission for God!"

I decided I'd have to give it more thought.

Andy already had one day's limit of sockeye's from the previous day at Kakhonak, but now, with the Newhalen River right there under our noses, and chock full of delicious, bright, fresh-from-the-ocean sockeye salmon, I had to admit: it *was* tough to dispute his reasoning. Besides, like Bob Cusack, Andy is a fairly polished gourmet cook, himself. It became evident there was simply no way Andy MacLeod was going to return home to Anchorage without having caught at least one more days' limit of salmon.

That was all the reason I needed to stay, too.

As table fare goes, sockeye salmon is generally regarded as being one of the most desired (if not *the* most desired) of the five species of pacific salmon. The last time I looked, if I remember correctly, reds were going for something well over $8 a pound back in the major grocery stores in town. All costs aside, just the smell of fine salmon filets sizzling over hot cottonwood bark coals is enough to warm the cockles of any true-blooded Alaskan's heart – especially during a cold winter's eve when the outside temperature's somewhere around minus ten degrees farenheit.

Ummm!

Andy and I got into sockeyes all right. One nearly always does fishing in mid July in the currents of the marvelous

Newhalen River at Iliamna, Alaska. The thing (besides the beautiful scenery) that makes it all so great is the way those Newhalen reds jump when they take a fly. And take a fly in the mouth they *do!* For some reason, those reds at the Newhalen are always some of the most acrobatic of any of the sockeyes I've ever encountered anywhere.

Skyrocketing sockeyes, they call 'em. To me, they're easily the strongest (pound for pound) fish of all five species of pacific salmon.

For those who have yet to experience Iliamna, there are actually *two* towns located in that area on the north shore of the lake. One is the town of *Iliamna*, itself, and the other is the village of *Newhalen*, a small settlement that exists 5 miles or so down the dirt road, just a half mile or so up from the mouth of the mighty Newhalen. Although the two villages are somewhat like suburbs existing in the same city – seperated only by a short distance – like most neighboring towns, the two are extremely competitive, especially during winter during basketball season from what I hear.

And, for those who might be wondering: *Yes*, there *is* a taxi service available in Iliamna, Alaska. Hang around at Iliamna Airport for an hour or so and you'll eventually see the taxi *van* rumble up in a cloud of dust. Just keep your eyes open for the little, dark-haired, smiling man in the maroon and mustard-colored 1974 Dodge van – the van with the half-crumpled roof with most of it's painting scraped off one side (enough so you can barely make it out). The writing's a bit difficult to make out, granted, but if you cock your head just right and squint your eyes just a bit you can make out the words:

"Jimmy's Iliamna Taxi."

Next day came quickly and it was suddenly time to return to Anchorage, even though the winds at Iliamna were fairly howling. To be honest, the last thing I wanted to do that gusty morning was crawl in the back of that tiny airplane and go flying-off into that howling gale, but fortunately, I've since forgotten most of the bumps, knocks, and very sincere prayers I muttered during that turbulent, 4 hour adventure back to town. Fortunately, the 'Cubs wings stayed on, and Andy did an impressive job of keeping his airplane off those imposing mountainsides we passed during our flight. When we finally landed at Merrill Field I congratulated Andy several times over on the excellent job of flying he'd done.

Each year, after fishing season has ended I'll tell myself: *"I'll think twice next time* before I go contorting my body into the backseat of a Super Cub and go flying off half-way across Alaska, battling brisk crosswinds and braving frightening downdrafts, risking life and limb to some forbidden mountainside somewhere, hoping to high heaven the wings stay on – all in the name of chasing Alaska's heavily spotted rainbow trout.

Then, the following spring I'll suddenly seem to remember the size and beauty of Alaska's beautiful rainbow trout and find myself hearing fly-fishing bells ringing off in the distance. That's when I'll say to myself: *"Okay. Maybe I will* – maybe just this one last time I'll contort my body into the backseat of a Super Cub – *but just this one last time* – just to get one more taste of Alaska's premier rainbow trout fly-fishing.

Fly-Fishing Adventure #8

The Talachulitna ...at Last
A Visit to TalStar Lodge

I'd been back in Anchorage only a week when I found myself getting anxious to get out hither and yon again. Fly-fishing in Alaska has a nasty habit of whetting my appetite for even more fly-fishing, I've learned. Consequently, I found myself ready to get my feet wet again, ready to get to the business of catching and releasing more of Alaska's trophy rainbow trout and char. That's when I glanced at my calendar and remembered that a very special trip was about to become a reality. What was coming was something I'd dreamed about for a long time.

Even though Eli was off fly-rodding for salmon at one of his secret spots, fly-fishing for salmon wasn't something I was too concerned about just then. Nope. Not me. I was dreaming of heavily spotted rainbows dancing at the end of *my* fly line. Better yet, I'd probably be seeing some in the near future, because I would soon be experiencing Alaska's marvelous Talachulitna River – after several years of waiting.

Craig Ketchum had wanted my fishing partner Tom Coomer and me to fly over to the Tal aboard his firm's deHavilland Turbo

Otter that sunny afternoon in early August , but things didn't
work out that way.

I had ridden in that souped-up floatplane before and I'd learned
it's quiet as a whisper and as fast as a dart. But as luck would
have it, one of the other passengers on our flight got delayed a bit,
so Craig ended up assigning the Turbo Otter to other duties
elsewhere. A half hour later Tom and I climbed aboard one of
Ketchum Air Service's standard, red, white and blue deHavilland
Beavers.

Ironically, this made me even happier. This way, with a slower
airplane, I'd have a little more time to relax and enjoy the view as
we passed over the Alaska wildreness. This way, I'd be able to
reflect a little bit more on the reality that I was *finally* going to
experience a river I'd waited several years to fish – Alaska's famed
Talachulitna River.

The *"Tal,"* they call it.

Over the years, I've had the good fortune to fish nearly fifty of
Alaska's premier rivers. But I'd waited nearly a decade to get my
first crack at the pretty Tal. It's not that I couldn't havefished the
river earlier; it's just that Alaska's other premier rivers kept
getting in the way. And yes, I'm aware of what they say,
"Sometimes waiting makes us appreciate things even more."

My mother still says things like that to me.

Charlie Pike was our pilot that afternoon. I'd flown with
Charlie several times over the years and I knew him to be an
expert bush pilot. Charlie's a real pro – always a gentleman,
always alert, and always courteous to his passengers. Things
people look for in a pilot.

Roger Bien (Craig Ketchum's assistant manager) had helped me put this particular trip together. As usual, Ketchum's service proved to be outstanding. When the big day finally arrived, Tom and I both drove seperate vehicles over to Lake Hood. When we arrived at Ketchum's we simply handed-over our car keys –they'd keep our vehicles safe and sound until we returned to Anchorage.

Let's go fishing!

I recalled that Evan Swensen (editor and publisher of *Alaska Outdoors* magazine) has long considered the Talachulitna one of his all-time favorite Alaska rivers – the very same river I'd read so much about in Jim Repine's books and magazine articles over the years. I must have read Jim's book, *Jim Repine's ALASKAN FISHING ADVENTURES* at least ten times. Chapter 7 deals solely with the famed Talachulitna River.

But, I asked myself, after all my study and reading and research and waiting, what did I know about the Tal?

For one thing, I'd heard that the rainbows there are supposedly a particularly colorful subspecie, with brilliant red stripes and fins and heavily spotted backs.

I'd also heard that the Tal is a somewhat temperamental stream at times, particularly susceptible to change caused by rains and storms. That's okay, I thought, "many great rivers are like that."

And I'd heard that rainbows are once again fairly plentiful at the Tal. Conflicting reports said that many of the rainbows had been decimated by those who refused to acknowledge catch and release. Fortunately, about ten years ago, the Alaska Department of Fish & Game deemed the Tal a total catch and release rainbow trout fishery.

I've often wondered, why isn't the entire state of Alaska a catch and release rainbow trout fishery? Would people starve to death if rainbows were designated off limits? If so, how many rainbows are these people killing?

Most people spoke of the Talachulitna River as being in a "state of rebuilding." Many say it's just now getting back to having the numbers of rainbows it had years ago, before people began clunking rainbows and tossing them in boxes for transportation back to the freezer or the garbage. Fortunately, anglers began to realize that the Tal is one of Alaska's world class rainbow fisheries.

Since the 'Tal is only about a 55 minute airplane ride from Anchorage, it offered an easy target:

"Let's go over and fill up a box of 'bows for the freezer, Harry!"

I'd inspected the Talachulitna River from the back seat of a slow, low-flying, single-engine bush plane before, but I'd never actually fished the river. "Heck, *everybody's* fished the Tal" people would say. Everybody but me. Consequently, fishing the Talachulitna became a virtual necessity – required to achieve my personal goal to experience each of Alaska's best rivers.

Earlier that season I'd fished with guide Ray Johnson over at Tony Sarp's Katmai Lodge, located on the Alagnak. In talking with Ray I learned that he'd guided on the Talachulitna for several years, working out of another lodge. It could tell that Ray had developed a genuine fondness for the Tal.

I was excited. I didn't exactly have to pinch myself – but finally, after ten years of waiting I was on my way.

We'd barely leveled off at approximately 2000 feet over Cook Inlet (on our way to the *real* Alaska) when I noticed Tom had fallen asleep. I could hardly believe it; we hadn't been in the air five minutes when his head started bobbing off to one side.

I don't mind if a fishing partner relaxes and enjoys himself, and grabs a little shuteye once in a while – but did Tom *have* to fall asleep almost during takeoff, on the very trip I'd waited several years to make?

Our destination was TalStar Lodge - one of only four or five lodges located at the famed Talachulitna River.

Our floatplane flight began over lowland flats and lakes and climbed up over the rolling slopes of Mt. Susitna, then over to the chocolate milk colored, silty glacial waters of the Skwentna River. There we made a river landing just downstream from where the crystal clear currents of the Tal enter in.

Lodge Manager Mike Patton and his assistant guide Gary Layton met us at the big Skwentna, where we'd hopped into TalStar's shiny new aluminum riverboat for the ten minute voyage to the Tal. From there, the trip to the lodge was only another five or six minutes. At the riverbank, we were met by another assistant on a 4-wheel drive ATV, who transported our baggage and gear up the path to the lodge.

Five minutes later Tom and I were shown to a newly-built, extremely clean, very comfortable two-man cabin. I liked the setup; we were located very near the river, so it was easy to walk over and fish after dinner. This proved to be a great advantage, especially to Tom, who's the kind of angler that is often referred to as a "fishaholic." At night we could open the windows and fall asleep to the music of the river.

Since it was early August we weren't too surprised to discover a few fresh silver (coho) salmon finning out in the river's glassy currents. The real surprise came when we discovered that a few kings were still present, along with a fair number of spawned-out red (or sockeye) salmon. An occasional pink salmon could be seen here and there, and of course, large, colorful rainbows were always nearby – whenever we could manage *not* to hook a salmon, instead.

I'd heard plenty over the years about the Tal being a great dry fly stream. Naturally, my first impulse was to tie on a dry. I tried a full assortment of dries, going through all the usual paces. Eventually I realized I was fishing with my heart and not my head. I switched to egg-patterns and began picking up fish. It was still simply too early for dry flies - just yet, anyway. "September will be better," Mike explained.

The next morning it was Tom who discovered the hot, working pattern for that time of year.

"What'd you catch it on?" I asked, but Tom pretended like he couldn't hear me. When I worked my way over to him and looked over his shoulder I saw that he was fishing a Flesh Fly - also called a Ginger Bunny Bug.

What? Flesh Flies?

To understand why Flesh Flies work, you have to understand the life cycle of the salmon, and "think" a little like a rainbow trout. Each year, salmon enter fresh water, spawn, die, and then slowly begin to decay and drift back downstream to the ocean -

becoming another hors d'oeurve in the ecosystem for rainbows and char to feed upon. Rainbows eagerly attack and devour this drifting, decaying salmon flesh as a natural offering. As the decaying flesh drifts downstream, it eventually lodges in the rocks and pea gravel, eventually serving as a future food source for many small organisms such as next spring's smolt and other, smaller organisms.

Tom showed me how he ties Flesh Flies. First, select a size-4 or size-2 hook, and then tie on a tan (or flesh colored) rabbit fur strip for the "body" and "wings," adding just a pinch or two of orange, or pink colored marabou, to create a *fleshy* color. Flesh Flies can be fished weighted or unweighted - depending upon the type of system you select to fish. Sinktip line delivery? Floating line delivery?

Tom decided to try the sinktip method, swinging a weighted flesh pattern along the Talachulitna's rocky bottom. The rainbows usually grab the swinging fly right on the turn, just when the fly looks as if is 'trying to get away.' Often, right at the swing, just at the last instant – that's when many rainbows will grab on and head for the moon.

You don't mind if I try a Flesh Fly, too, do you, old buddy? I asked. "You don't happen to have a couple of spares I could borrow, do you?"

Tom and I found the Tal to be very wadable, pretty, and extremely enjoyable; reminding me of a typical western U.S., blue-ribbon trout stream. And, yes, the rainbows there did indeed turn out to be surprisingly stunning, with ultra-brilliant red stripes and very red front, or caudal fins. While we were there the water of the Tal was extremely clear, just like I'd always imagined it would be, but we did learn that the 'Tal can be moody and fairly temperamental at times.

She's a finicky but very lovely lady, the Tal!

One evening, after a dinner of grilled steaks and fried chicken, Mike Patton and I stood fishing about a mile or so upstream from the lodge, not fishing awfully hard really, just allowing our lines to dangle in the currents as we chatted. Tom and Gary were fishing across from us, over on another gravel bar, probing the riffles on their side of the river.

I'd just switched from a Light Hendrickson (a fly that hadn't been working) to a very large, size-6 Steelhead Bee pattern (a fly I'd chosen at random while rummaging through my fly box). For years I'd liked the looks of this fly but I'd never selected it before.

Mike was interested in the bamboo fly rod I was carrying that evening, so I'd just handed it over to him to try out. It's a Charlie Jenkins 2-piece, a 4-weight, a 7-footer, a 2-tip beauty I'd obtained in a trade with Len Codella at Heritage Sporting Goods back east. Anyway, there we were, just enjoying the evening, just standing there talking, allowing our flies to simply bounce on the river's surface in the swirling currents. All of a sudden a loud GULP and SPLASH broke the stillness and caused both Mike and me to turn and stare in disbelief.

It took a few moments for us to realize what our eyes had just seen.

Did you just see what I just saw?!" I muttered after I'd finally regained my breath.

Yes, I sure as hell did!" Mike admitted sheepishly.

We had barely caught sight of a huge rainbow's head just as it disappeared back into the riffles, and with that size-6 Steelhead Bee stuck in the corner of it's mouth.

"You've got him, Mike!!" I hollered.

Sure enough, *my* cane rod (the rod now in Mike's hand) had suddenly doubled over, the line very taut.

While we'd stood there talking a huge rainbow (we estimated the creature to be at least ten-pounds and probably bigger) had slowly approached the big, surly-looking dry fly, given into its basic predator instincts, and savegely attacked the big fly. Naturally, when it climbed aboard, *my* bamboo rod was in Mike's hand.

But the action didn't last very long. With a loud TWING that sounded like a small bore rifle going off, the huge rainbow snapped the tapered leader and vanished. My bamboo rod suddenly straightened as if nothing had happened.

I looked at Mike, who was standing there with his mouth hanging open. Suddenly I wondered if we'd both merely imagined the experience. Obviously, the 4X leader I'd been fishing that evening was entirely unworthy of holding such an honorable fish for more than a fraction of a second.

"Did you just see what I think I saw?" I gasped to Mike a second time, "or am I just imagining things?"

"Man, what a rainbow trout that was!" Mike exclaimed. Where in the heck did something like that come from?" he mused aloud. "The water there is only about nine inches deep."

We had just received a fishing lesson of a lifetime. Apparently, that big rainbow could not refuse that big Steelhead Bee pattern.

Bobbing in the riffles, that fly must have looked like a large hornet or a moth or a wasp fluttering at the surface – a sight obviously too enticing for any self respecting rainbow to resist. But then, you know what they say about selecting flies: "Choose large flies for large fish...Small flies for smaller fish." That's the theory at least, although it doesn't always work out that way.

But for the most part, I'm willing to agree with it. So is Mike Patton at Alaska's TalStar Lodge.

Even though we'd been treated to one of nature's unusual phenomena that evening, dry-fly fishing the Talachulitna during early August wasn't exactly what I'd pictured. It was simply too early, what with all the loose, drifting salmon eggs and decaying salmon flesh drifting about in the currents.

We noticed at least four species of salmon still finning in the river's lower currents. As most readers will instinctively know, egg or flesh patterns are usually required to hook rainbows regularly at many of Alaska's rivers during August.

The next morning Tom Coomer proved the flesh pattern worked wonders. He'd beaten me to the river and was catching rainbows one after another. After noticing him fishing a sinktip, I didn't waste a minute changing spools over from a floater and switching to a weighted Flesh Fly.

It was a good thing Tom had stayed up the night before and tied up several for us.

Before we knew it, our Talachulitna journey was over. The following morning we motored down to to mouth where Tom Noble picked us up in Ketchum's Turbo-Beaver and returned us to 'civilization.'

Claire Dubbin and Mike Patton's TalStar Lodge had provided a very relaxing, rustic, and refreshing fly-fishing experience, with great food and good company. Its close proximity to the river reminded me a lot of the summer cabin I'd enjoyed as a teenager while growing up in the The Rockies.

And the Tal? Well, she's a lovely lady slightly out of place in the rough and tumble Alaska setting she's found. She's a jewel of a river, and deserves all the respect she's famous for. Many famous and not so famous visitors have traveled far and wide just to taste her sweetness over the years, and most of them have fallen in love with her during their stays.

As far as I'm concerned, Jim Repine was absolutely right a decade earlier when he proclaimed, "If ever there was a river that deserves to be designated as a rainbow trout catch and release water, Alaska's Talachulitna River is that place."

I can only hope future visitors will revere and respect the lovely Talachulitna River for what she is, for she truly is a world class rainbow trout stream, flowing so pretty there through those thick Alaska ferns.

Fly-Fishing Adventure #9

Kenai Drift for Big 'bows
with Alaska Troutfitters

I'd been standing around, just shooting the bull with Greg Lindgren over at the *Rod and Reel* when the front door suddenly opened and a man with a orange-colored beard entered and made his way to the rear of the flyshop. I watched him through the corner of my eye as he headed directly for the the leader tippet material department.

Here was a man who was clearly on a mission. By the look in his eye I could tell he was a fly-fisher who had no time to waste fooling around examining rods or turning handles on expensive reels. No time to waste standing around chatting, dreaming of future days fighting big fish. Here was a fly-fisher who was clearly in a hurry to get on with the business of selecting a leader tippet material of undisputed quality.

Somehow this bearded man looked vaguely familiar to me. But for the life of me I couldn't remember where I'd seen him before.

Where do I know him from? I kept asking myself.

Squinting my eyes and straining to recall, I soon forgot what Greg and I had been talking about.

I racked my brain for an answer – to no avail.

Something about this bearded stranger told me he was extremely fishwise. No, more than fishwise; this fisherman reeked of being experienced. No question about it; this fly-fishing gentleman carried an undeniable air of angling wisdom about him. His eyes told the story of a man who'd logged hundreds of hours fly-fishing for Alaska's biggest rainbows. One look told me he was a man who'd landed and released many monstrous fish.

I interrupted my conversation with Greg as politely as possible and slowly made my way to the rear of the shop. He was still there, all right, carefully examining the small, colorfully-packaged plastic spools of coiled monofiliment hanging on the wall.

"What do you think of *such and such* brand of leader material compared to *so and so* brand?" he asked.

Was he talking to *me?*

"Do you prefer brand X or brand Z?" the voice said again.

When I turned I saw the bearded man was looking right at me.

(Somehow I sensed this fly-fishing mystery man *already* knew more about leader tippet materials than I'd ever know, yet apparently he was savvy enough to want to pick my brain and see if (1) I *did* happen to know anything about tippet material brands that he might not, and (2) if I knew anything about *anything*.

"Excuse me," I said "But before I give you my ideas, I must ask you, because you look so darn familiar; "Where in the heck do I know you from?"

"Name's Bob. Pleased to meet you" he replied, extending his hand.

"Nice to meet you, *too*, Bob," I said, as my mind asked the obvious question: Bob who?

Long seconds ticked by before I finally had to ask again.

"Excuse me" I said. "Could you be kind enough to tell me your *last* name? Maybe that'll remind me where I know you from – I'm *sure* I know you from somewhere, but I just can't place it – not exactly, anyway."

"Trout," the man replied. "Bob Trout."

That was it! BOB TROUT! Finally, a name to fit the face.

Suddenly I realized I was speaking face to face with one of the most experienced rainbow trout fishermen in all Alaska. Yet, here he was, asking *me* about tipper materials...

"*Yes!* Bob TROUT! That's it!" I said. "*You're* that fly-fisher that fishes down on the Kenai all the time, the one everybody always talks about!"

By this time my mind had begun to recall many of the photographs I'd seen of this rainbow man – each of them showing a fly-fisherman displaying trophy rainbow trout and char. His was the face I'd seen in so many pictures all over town; beautiful, color photos of a fly-fisher holding up football-sized and larger rainbows – rainbows much larger than anything I'd ever taken – rainbows and Dollies in the 15 to 17 pound range.

And always, the fisherman in those photos wore an old, weatherbeaten cap with TROUT embroidered above the brim.

"Well, Bob Trout, I must ask you, *Why* are you asking *me* about leader tippets? After all, *you're* the one who's landed hundreds of trophy fish high up in the record class over the years – that is, unless I'm mistaking you with someone else ...and I don't think I am."

Before Bob could reply, I found myself speaking again.

Surprised at the suddenness of my own words I said, "I'd like to fish with you this season if I may...I'd like to learn what it is you know about catching Alaska's trophy Kenai River rainbows that I don't know... things that I simply haven't a clue about... and I'd like to get to know a fellow named Bob Trout a little better, too, if I may."

"You're welcome to come fishing with Curt or me anytime you'd like," Bob Trout finally got a word in. "But I doubt very much if I can teach you much," he continued.

Teach me much?! *Was he crazy?*

Truth be known, I'd have been honored just to carry his fly rod – pleased as punch just to have the opportunity to watch him fish.

"Like I've said," I responded, "*I've seen* all those pictures of you holding those monster rainbows down on the Kenai. "*I'd* be the one getting the fishing lesson, trust me!" I assured him.

That's when Bob pulled a business card from his front pocket and handed it to me.

ALASKA TROUTFITTERS, it read. Then it went on to list all the usual stuff: Guided float trips, Affordable, Kenai River drifts, Rentals... Photography... Sightseeing... Full Day or Half-

Day Trips... the usual sort of stuff. The difference was, I realized Bob Trout wasn't the usual sort of guide.

Thanking Bob for his card I tucked it away in my wallet for safe keeping. It'd be a business card I'd take good care of – not one of those cards that always somehow end up in the waste basket.

That's when I shared with Bob my belief that brand *such and such* leader tippet material is probably manufactured by brand *so and so*, anyway. There was no basis for my theory, really; I'd come up with that conclusion totally on my own, only by closely examining and comparing packaging and labeling, noticing very similar plastic spools that had caught my attention. Not only that, both brands of mono used the same *type* styles on their labels, even though the labels had been printed on different colored paper.

Bob's eyes widened as he listened intently. After all, ascertaining the minute details pointing to the finest leader tippet material is important stuff to a serious fly-fishermen like Mr. Bob Trout.

"You know, I think you might be right!" Bob exclaimed. "Not only that, but brand X is a little less expensive than brand Z. *And here* I've been using brand Z for all these years! They certainly had *me* fooled." he said. "I feel like a real dummy!"

"A....excuse me, but a...," I tried to get a word in.

"You know," Bob continued, "I'll bet you're right. I'll bet both of these brands *are* made by the same manufacturer!"

From the look Bob Trout gave me you'd have thought I was a virtual fly-fishing tackle genius just then, but little did he know I'd all but exausted my entire knowledge regarding monofilament and leader tippet marerials.

I *was* only guessing, of course, but it was something I'd wondered about from time to time. And besides, if my theory was good enough for Bob Trout, it must be the same leader tippet material found on both of those two, very cleverly-disguised plastic spools.

After another long pause Bob said, "You know, I haven't the foggiest idea why I didn't ever think of that..." he said, wearing a look of amazement. Then he spent a few moments quietly examining the two different brands.

"You can come fishing with me anytime you'd like to." Bob's words surprised me. "I like the way you think, Dan, but please, quit calling me Mr. Trout, will ya? "Please, Just call me Bob."

I sneeked a quick peek at Greg who was standing over by the counter. He was busy pretending he was straightening up some items but I could tell by the smile on his face that Greg'd probably overheard most of our conversation. The way Bob and I'd been talking, he'd have had to.

The smile on Greg's face told me he'd gotten a chuckle out our fascinating, if less than scientific discussion.

So, speaking like a gloating adolescent might, and looking directly at Greg I said in a boisterous voice, "Sounds like I"ll be getting a fishing lesson from Bob Trout one of these first days,

Greg! Care to join me— and maybe get a fishing lesson from Bob Trout *personally?*"

Greg's smile widened but his response pretty well summed things up: "To tell you the truth, I get a fishing lesson from Bob Trout just about everytime he comes into this shop" he said, flashing another big grin. "But you're right about one thing: In my opinion, Bob Trout is one of the most experienced rainbow trout fly-fishers in all Alaska! "In fact," Greg continued, "many of this shop's clients have talked of Bob's magic with a fly rod on several occasions. . . My guess is that we'd all do well to listen to what Bob Trout has to say."

I glanced over at Bob, who was obviously embarrassed. Bob's the shy, humble type, so by this time he was ready to change the subject.

Slowly, Greg left the front counter and ambled over to the rear of the shop and pointed to a framed picture hanging on the back wall, above a rack of bamboo fly rods. It was a photograph I'd somehow always managed to overlook.

The 8 X 12 color photograph showed a short, red-haired man with an orangish beard displaying a huge, heavily-spotted but very much alive rainbow trout. The fish was so big and chunky that I immediately found myself wondering what strength and brand of leader tippet material it took to land such a fish. The rainbow in that photo had to have weighed at least eighteen or nineteen pounds. The man holding the fish had a distinct twinkle in his eye. Not surprisingly, he looked quite a bit like the shy man standing right next to me.

Two days later I telephoned Bob Trout at his Windbreaker Restaurant in Wasilla, a town located north of Anchorage on the Parks Highway just 35 miles and about 30 minutes by automobile distant.

"Dan," Bob said when he answered, "I looked at the schedule and, unfortunately, I've got to work up here at the restaurant for a couple of days. Then, following that, I've got to drive down to Troutfitters down in Cooper Landing and hold down the office Thursday thru Sunday (it's Curt's turn to go fishing for a while) but I've talked to Curt, and he's anxious to meet you at the Alpine Inn Motel in Cooper Landing at about one o'clock next Thursday if you think can make it. "I think Curt mentioned something about a couple of spinfishermen scheduled to go out earlier that morning, but after that he'll be ready to drift for big rainbows with you, later that afternoon. Why don't you give him a call and set things up? I hate missing a week of fishing due to work, but you and I can go out fishing on another day – maybe in a couple of weeks from now, after the weather cools down a bit and we can really get serious about hooking into some big fish. How does around the middle of September sound?"

"September sounds fine," I answered, "but it's *you* that I'm really wanting to go out fishing with, Bob" I continued. "I'd be happy to simply wait for our trip, or, if you'd like, I can drive down to Cooper Landing and meet this Curt fellow next Thursday, whatever you recommend, Bob. . . By the way, what's Curt's last name?" I asked.

"TROUT." Bob said flatly. "CURT Trout."

Naturally, this second invitation came as welcomed news, although I *did* feel a bit disappointed about not going out with Bob Trout, personally. It looked like I'd just have to wait for that trip.

Yet, in another way, maybe TWO Trouts would be better than one' I thought, "..especially if this Curt Trout fellow turned out to be as personable as Bob.

I thanked Bob and explained I'd wait to hear from him regarding our upcoming fishing trip together. But I had to admit, I was a little excited about getting to know this Curt Trout fellow too, whoever he was.

Had to be a brother, I figured.

Thursday finally rolled around and I was there all right– there being the Alpine Inn Motel located just up the road and across the street from my friend, Mark Wilson's, *Hamilton's Place* in Cooper Landing.

Hamilton's Place is a famaliar old haunt for me, a four-star hamburger and gasoline stop featuring good, homecooked food and an exceptionally fine view of the Kenai. Over the years I'd stopped there on several occasions – meeting friends or stopping for a bit before hitting the road again for the long, two-hour drive back to Anchorage. Hamilton's has always been a great place to fill 'er up and grab a bite of apple pie or a cheeseburger – a pretty place to take a breather, drain the radiator, and say hello or bid farewell to the river.

When I pulled up at the Alpine Inn a nice lady named Rosemary and her husband, Richard, were waiting for me behind the motel counter. They explained that Curt Trout would be waiting for me down by the river, down at a boat launching area called, *Sportsman's Landing,* just another couple of miles farther down the highway. Rosemary said she'd put together a lunch for Curt and me. *That* was a nice touch and a real surprise.

"Well, at least let me pick up a six-pack of diet soda, please."

For sale under the front counter was an unusually fine assortment of single egg patterns; quality, hand-tied flies in several different colors. These flies had obviously been prepared under the direction of Bob and/or Curt Trout. There had to be at least nine or ten different shades of glo-bugs to select from – everything from light creme and champagne to black.

Someone obviousluy had gone to a great deal of trouble to tie-up all those egg patterns. The assortment represented a color for any of the myriad of fishing situations found down on the Kenai, depending on the time of year and the salmon runs. Selling flies to the sport fishing trade is a common practice down on the river – always big business in southcentral Alaska, and particularly the Kenai Peninsula, even though most of the fly stops down that way couldn't begin to compare with the selection I saw at the Alpine Inn.

"I guess you two must be the parents of Bob and Curt Trout" I said, but Richard was already halfway out of the office door on his way to an errand, and Rosemary had just reached to answer the phone .

Thanks again for the lunch, Rosemary!" I hollered through the screen door as I waived goodbye and scurried to the Blazer. A glance at my watch had told me I'd better get moving. . .

Curt Trout was waiting for me.

A glance at my watch had told me it was 1:00 p.m. –right on the dot– an unusual, lucky occurrence for me, especially considering the road construction I'd had to negotiate on the drive down from Anchorage. Usually, that trip only requires about an hour and forty-five minutes, but this day the extra half-hour or so I'd allowed had delivered me right on time.

I made a mental note to return to the Alpine Inn soon. It'd make a comfortable, affordable place for me and a companion to overnight later in September when the rainbow trout fishing down at the Kenai started to get serious.

Four minutes later I pulled into the parking area at Sportsman's and, sure enough, there was Curt Trout, standing by his driftboat, smiling – welcoming me just like we were old friends who hadn't seen each other in years.

Curt seemed a little younger than Bob; whats more, the two didn't really look all that much alike. One thing was for sure, though, one glance at Curt Trout told me I was about to receive a big river fly-fishing lesson from a very experienced professional.

"I'm ready to go whenever you are, Dan!" Curt greeted me with a smile, adding, "The rainbows and char were biting good down here this morning, and I think we're about to hook into a couple of ten or twelve pounders this afternoon, especially if the water keeps warming up like it's been doing. River's been running fairly deep with the runoff and all, but now that the sun's been out for a couple days I've got a feeling we're in for a great afternoon's fishing!"

I liked Curt's style. His was the positive kind of attitude that can set the mood for an entire afternoon, regardless if the day's success ratio turned out to be anything close to expectations. I'd learned long ago that in fly-fishing, it's not how many fish you catch, so much as who you're with that really counts, after all is said and done. Not only that, but I'm superstitious about fly-fishing. Seems the less I try to be too serious about the sport the more success I have.

Reaching for my old 9-foot 8-weight battle stick, along with a beloved, 9 1/2-foot 6-weight (a rod that has become one of my pride and joy fishing tools of late) I hurriedly uncased two Hardy Marquise-6 reels (one with a 6/7 floater and one with an 8-weight floater) and slipped into a pair of 3-mill neoprene waders. Grabbing the six-pack of diet Coke, I laced-up my "boat" (tennis) shoes, slammed the tailgate to the Blazer, and rushed over to the drift boat where Curt was holding out his hand.

"By the way, Curt" I said, "I just want you to know that I don't really care too much if we catch a lot of record fish today or not" I said, as we shook hands.

"For me," I went on, "just getting out of the city for a few hours and being able to spend some time out fishing in this grand Alaska setting is all the payoff I could ever ask for."

Then, stealing a sideways glance at the snow-capped peaks behind us, I added, "Like you, Curt, I must have viewed this beautiful river valley and these mountains a hundred times before, but somehow I never get tired of seeing it. It never becomes old, know what I mean?"

Couldn't agree more," Curt answered. "I've been guiding down here on the Kenai going on three years now, and every day that I drift the river I appreciate it as much as I did the first time I laid eyes on it," he added.

"Saw a 2-year old bull moose standing down river over by the whirlpool hole just the other evening. Prettiest sight you ever saw." Curt said. "He was all alone, posing there on the banks of the world famous Kenai River, all silhouetted against a foggy mist."

I hurried to grab a seat in the front of the driftboat as Curt shoved us off for the adventure that lay ahead. Above, a Bald Eagle soared in a nearly cloudless sky. Just downstream was the little peninsula that marks the confluence of the Kenai and the Russian.

As I always do whenever I see that spot, I pictured Lee Wulff and his father standing there, casting at that very point where those two great rivers converge. Years later, Lee wrote about that trip he made as a youngster with his father – and a guide named Henry Skilak – to that spot where the two great rivers meet. But, suddenly, that was seventy years ago, and now, sadly, Lee Wulff has moved on to other waters. Still, everytime I pass that spot I can't help but imagine Lee and his father just standing there casting, enjoying their time together, fly-fishing for Alaska's trophy rainbows.

Lee Wulff described that spot later as being, '...one of the finest fshing spots in all of Alaska."

Just what is it about fly-fishing that seems to make time stand still ?' I found myself wondering.

But now it was time to get to fishing. So I quickly tied a size-8 glo-bug to the extra, 2-foot tippet section I'd added to my tapered 9-foot 2X leader, using a surgeon's knot to make the splice. Above the knot I pinched on a size-3 split shot (a larger than normal split shot) that I hoped would be about the right size to deliver the fly to the correct depth in the fast flowing Kenai.

By employing the services of a full-floating line, I'd still be able to mend at the surface. This allows a deeply drifted fly to bounce and bob in the currents –much as a natural egg does.

I watched as Curt worked the oars, speeding us across the Kenai's heavy currents over to the other side of the river – just below where the pretty Russian flows in.

"We'll do *some* fishing while we drift" Curt said, "but I've found the best fishing stopping at gravel bars and islands, then getting out and working the riffles on foot. You fished the Kenai much in the past, Dan?" Curt asked.

"Well, Yes – a little," I replied, "but not like *some* guys I know. Oh, I've fiddled around here and there on the Kenai on several occasions, but officially speaking I've only drifted this upper section of the river maybe four or five times. Suddenly, that's been three or four years ago, now." I admitted. I *have* fished a bit here and there for lakers, reds, and for a few rainbows over at Skilak, over by Russ and Jeanie's cabin, but, to tell you the truth, I continued, "I guess I haven't concentrated on the Kenai too seriously because of my concerns of simply finding too many people fishing down on the big river."

"From what I've overheard from others," Curt said, "quite a few people feel that same way about fishing the Kenai at first. That is, *until* they get into one of our Troutfitter's drift boats and see parts of the river where you'd swear no man has ever set foot before" he winked, then continued, "Hopefully we'll get that same feeling this afternoon, unless, of course, a big ugly cloudburst develops and ruins this little drift of ours. But, by the way the skies look right now, though, I don't really see that happening."

By this time we were almost over to the other bank. Suddenly, a fish struck my fly and began a powerful, twisting fight, sounding deep into the river's main currents. I could tell it was a Dolly Varden char right from the 'take' by the way my rod's tip pulsed and bobbed – always a sure sign of a Dolly.

When we reached the other bank I jumped out, fumbling for the reel handle of my old, Hardy Marquise#6 reel. Eventually I took up slack, but that chunky, 4-pound Dolly had taken out almost half of the 100 or so yards of 30-lb backing on the spool before I was able to gain control.

At times, the Kenai's swift currents can surprise an angler, especially during times of high water like we were experiencing that day. Add a solid fish to that picture, and you've got all the challenge and excitement a fly-fisher could ask for.

Eventually I worked the char over to me. Reaching out with my free hand I gently grasped the pretty green and orange spotted Dolly by the tail, while I rummaged for my forceps with the other

155

hand. Ever so gently, I removed the hook from the fish's lower lip. After a couple of minutes the Dolly was revived and released – to fight again another day.

"Nice way to begin the afternoon, Dan!" Curt shouted from the gravel bank. "What color glo-bug were you using? I need to know because the fish around here seem to change their minds regarding color preferrence almost hourly!"

"Apricot," I shouted back.

What I didn't bother telling Curt was that apricot is often the only color glo-bug I reach for, no matter what time of year it may be. I have no real justification for this habit – just good 'ol superstition, mostly. But I had to admit, fishing an apricot glo-bug has seemed to work more magic for me than the other colors I've fished over the seasons.

The rest of the afternoon was spent hopscotching to various islands and gravel banks. Curt suddenly started hooking fish on a regular basis, employing his "big river nymphing technique," a nymphing method I'd never seen before. Oh, I was familiar with standard nymphing, all right, but I quickly learned there is nymphing and there is *nymphing*, and Curt Trout quickly proved to be a master of this new, big river technique. He began picking-up fish after fish in a very methodical fashion.

I'd catch a rainbow, or two, and Curt would catch and release five or six.

The basis of Curt's and Bob's 'big river technique' is fishing a floating line, using an oversized strike indicator. Where I was used to the small, brightly-colored, self-adhesive, folding-type indicators, Curt Trout amazed me by fishing a strike indicator nearly the size of a ping pong ball. Below the indicator he'd use about a 12-foot long tapered leader, ending with a 2X (or 10lb) 2-foot tippet section, secured by using either a surgeon's or a blood knot. Above the knot he'd place what he estimated to be the correct amount of split shot for the water he was facing, and of course, at the end of the rig he tied on a single-egg pattern – the color carefully selected according to an intricate system Curt and Bob had worked-out over the seasons according to "the hatch."

The theory behind Curt's big river technique seemed flawless, "Dollies and rainbows are obviously keying in on loose, drifting salmon eggs – so the entire principle seems to be to duplicate a natural, downstream sunken drift as closely as possible."

"To accomplish this," Curt went on, "use a floating line. Sink tips won't do the job, simply because it's the very narure of a sinking line presentation to drag or 'swing' the fly across the bottom in an unnatural way. Conversely, using a floating line for nymphing allows an egg-pattern to nearly duplicate a *natural, downstream* drift. In order to fish big, deep, swift-moving water, an angler requires a larger than normal stike indicator to know when to set the hook at a strike."

"That reminds me of one other thing, too" Curt said. "A 'dry fly' (or upward) strike is not usually very effective when fishing this method. Striking upward will only pull the fly out of the fish's mouth."

"What You've Got To Remember Is: Form a big, intentional loop on the surface, and, when the indicator moves, *Strike Downstream*, utilizing the water tension at the surface to effectively pull the line *upstream*, thus pulling the hook into the corner of the fish's mouth. Remember to feed out a big, wide, intentional loop at the surface when first casting, then feed out lots of additional line while you watch the drifting strike indicator closely.

When the indicator wiggles – Strike! Downstream!"

Sounds simple, right?

It wasn't *that* difficult to learn to strike sideways when the water I fished was moving from left to right. But right to left proved to be a different matter completely.

Why? Well, in the first place, at the instant of the strike, muscle memory tells the fisherman to strike upward. Then, after a microsecond's hesitation and readjustment, a fairly decent strike can sometimes be salvaged. But when striking away from the 'power zone' a slight lack of coordination can result in a less than effective strike – thus missing the fish.

Simple, right?

After discovering this, I decided that from that moment on, at least while learning this new system, I'd try and fish only left to right flowing waters – allowing my muscle memory some advantage, at least. Once in every three or four times I'd manage to hook a fish, but usually I was either too late, or I hadn't even seen the strike indicator twitch. "Ooops, you missed it" Curt would say.

"*Missed What?*" I'd say back.

It was amazing to watch Curt Trout when it came to noticing strikes and hooking fish. Someone could argue that after fishing the Kenai for three years Curt *should* be good – but good isn't the word – Curt Trout was amazing to watch, to say the least.

"Curt, I've got a question to ask you" I said as he was releasing yet another fish. *"Who's better? Curt Trout or Bob Trout?"*

A broad smile came to Curt's face and he said, "Well, to tell you the truth, we're both about the same. We both still learn things everyday we fish, but Bob's definitely luckier than I am. I might catch a few more fish than Bob at times, but somehow, it's Bob Trout who usually winds up with the really big rainbows."

Before I knew it, it was nearing six o'clock in the evening. Curt and I had nearly finished our drift. We were just upstream from Jim's Landing, the exit point for an Upper Kenai drift.

In a last-ditch effort, I dragged an egg-pattern behind the boat while Curt worked the oars, keeping us over to the right in the channel, where we'd be able to cross over in the Kenai's main currents.

Suddenly, I felt a heavy take and my rod nearly doubled over. My old Hardy reel began to whine and give line. "Looks like you've hooked a late season sockeye" Curt said, "possibly a jack."

"A *what?*" I said.

"Yeah, sockeyes have jacks, too – just like king salmon do. You know, immature males that re enter fresh water, following mature fish on their upstream miggrations to spawn."

"August 27 is a little late for sockeyes, isn't it?"

"Sometimes the sockeye jacks re enter the river a second time, later in the season," he answered.

159

Sure enough, after a strong, five-minute battle against the river's main currents, I brought the fish to hand just as Curt maneuvered the driftboat into Jim's Landing.

"It's a sockeye jack, all right!" Curt said smiling.

"*How did you know* it was a sockeye all along? And better, yet, *a jack?*"

"Your rod tip was *acting* like you'd hooked a sockeye."

On my drive back to Anchorage, after thanking Curt Trout for a great day's fishing, I found myself wondering about Alaska's professional fishing guides. 'How can they tell one specie from another judging from how a rod tip behaves?' I asked myself.

Certainly one of the great mysteries of the universe, as far as I'm concerned.

But as the miles slipped by the thing I found myself thinking about most was the 'big water nymphing technique' I'd learned from Curt Trout that afternoon. I'd witnessed some fairly amazing fishing feats in my life, but none more wondrous than Curt Trout hooking rainbows and char forty to fifty yards downstream by watching a bobbing strike indicator that, at that distance, looks more like the head of a pin – that's *if* you can even see the thing that far away.

I decided to follow up on a chance at an upcoming drift with Bob Trout. Bob might be *as good* as Curt, I thought, but certainly, he couldn't fish any better than Curt Trout had.

Could he?

Just maybe I'd pull-out my Teeny T-300 and challenge Bob Trout to a deep river fly-fishing showdown.

Fly-Fishing Adventure #10

KULIK LODGE

Rainbows Royale

Suddenly it had turned late August in Alaska. Summer was slipping by entirely too quickly. Something – don't ask me what – just wasn't right. I don't know, I just had *this feeling*.

Try as I may I couldn't put a finger on it. Sure, the Major League Baseball strike was in full swing – who would've ever imagined Matt Williams, Frank Thomas, and Ken Griffey, Jr. all cut off right in the middle one of the hottest home run races in history? And, my old favorite, Tom Watson, hadn't been sinking too many putts of late. But there had to be another reason.

Yes, my advertising business in Anchorage remained fairly steady – *steady pressure and deadlines, that is*. To put it mildly, I wasn't exactly having the time of my life just then, even though I live in Alaska, the very place that is known for its sensational summers, supreme scenery, and fantastic fly-fishing. Something was definitely askew, I realized – *but what?*

Then I picked up a copy of the local newspaper, *The Anchorage Daily News*. Bosnia was still...the economy looked down...Crime was up...Watson was hitting greens but still not... and, to compound the matter, that was about the time I began to notice that I couldn't read fine print like I used to.

Worse, only the day before I'd received a notice from G. Loomis, Inc., explaining that they were temporarily back ordered on the new 9-foot 4-weight, state-of-the-art GLX fly rod I'd ordered. *Great* – just what I needed, another reason for a full blown anxiety attack.

Then I began to realize that in only six more short weeks snow could begin falling (it always snows in Anchorage during mid October, it seems). *That* didn't exactly have me jumping for joy, believe me.

Then Eli called – really putting the icing on the cake. "They're nailing rainbows like crazy down at the Russian and hammering 'em on the Upper Kenai," he said.

Something was telling me it was time to go fly-fishing again.

It wasn't as if I hadn't picked up a fly rod a time or two already that season, but after thinking about it some more, I decided maybe it *really was* time I get out of the city for a couple of days. Either that, or check in over at the local, *'or get help somewhere.'*

After all, it was summer in Alaska. I was *supposed* to be having fun, right? Just because already three of summer's four months had quickly slipped by didn't mean I...

That's when it hit me.

I'd obviously picked-up a case of, 'the fever.'

Rainbowitis I call it.

Just where, I did not know, but I'd obviously contracted it and I'd experienced similar attacks in other years, so I *knew*. This time I realized I was experiencing not only a craving for fly-fishing, but a craving for a particular place. It reminded me of the feeling you get when it's late at night and you realize you've got to get up and get dressed and drive across town to Bob's Drive Inn for a superburger deluxe. Sure, you *could* pull into the neighborhood *Donald's* located just around the corner, but somehow, the trip across town to Bob's is probably worth it because not just any old superburger will do.

After thinking about it a little, I realized I was experiencing a craving for a place they call Kulik. Some people call it KEWluck, and others call it KOOlick – but even though the correct pronounciation is, "QUELICK," any way you care to pronounce it, Kulik definitely means premier to this fly-fisher. In my humble opinion, along with my beloved Alagnak, Kulik is simply one of the places in Alaska that qualifies as "Rainbow Heaven." In the native tongue, Kulik means, "Upper Lake." As I understand, it is also a Ukranian surname.

Nevertheless, Kulik ranks *right up there* – not only with the Alagnak – but with the Agulawok, with Lower Talarik, with that little 'secret' stream Tom Bukowski and I fly into every once in a while, and with Brooks as being one of the finest rainbow spots in the state. That's saying quite a bit, I realize, and it excludes the Kenai and other famed Alaska rivers (the Goodnews and the Kanektok included) but all things considered, I'll stand by that statement. Simply put, Kulik means *rainbows* in Alaskanese.

I decided it was time I called Katmailand, Inc., headquartered at Lake Hood in Anchorage.

When the phone rang, Kip Minnery (Sonny Petersen's right hand man) answered. After the customary preliminaries I came right to the point.

"Kip, I really need to make reservations for two over at Kulik – A.S.A.P. – for a couple of days if there's *any* space at all available. Think you can help?"

"Let me talk with Sonny," Kip said, "I'll try and reach him over at King Salmon where he's assisting with flying tourists from the Naknek over to Brooks. Sonny'll know if there's any space at all available over at Kulik. Then, soon as I talk with him, I'll try and call you back, maybe later this afternoon or first thing tomorrow morning. I'll let you know how things look."

"Thanks, Kip!" I said. "I really appreciate it, and I'll be anxiously awaiting your call." Little did he know *how* anxiously.

I'd fished over at Katmailand's Kulik Lodge on other occasions, so I was already aware of what a fabulous dry fly water the place it is. Somehow I knew it'd be the perfect solution for my fairly advanced case of, 'Rainbowitis.' I'd tried to fight it alone once, earlier, had even attempted abstinence once – but it just didn't work.

Fortunately for me, Kip called me down at the advertising office the very next day. "You're in luck" he said, "I was able to reach Sonny and he's confirmed there's room enough for two fishermen for two days over at Kulik this coming Saturday."

Kip went on to say something about bringing a partner and flying over with John Siegel in Katmailand's Navajo Twin, and fishing for rainbows with head guide, Wayne Hansen. Then he teased me, saying about there being too many rainbows infiltrating the rivers over that way and them needing help thinning 'em out.

"It'll be a tough assignment, Kip, but my partner and I will be there on Saturday and we'll see what we can do." I responded. "Please thank Sonny for me again if you talk to him, and thanks to *you*, Kip!"

My wife didn't know it yet, but come Saturday morning, I was going fishing. After all, I rationalized, this was a medically-warranted, mental health related trip.

Besides, like Kip had noticed, I'd contracted a bonafide case of *the fever*.

I decided it was time I called John Staser over at Mountain View Sports in Anchorage. John's a real gentleman, a fly-fisher extraordinaire, a man, who, like me, really appreciates rainbow trout on dry flies. John would make a worthy companion for a trip like this one.

Even though the surface winds were blowing steadily at 15 to 20 knots on Saturday, John Siegel, our pilot, said the weather was entirely "manageable." "No problem," he added, "we'll probably be cruising over to Kulik at somewhere around 12,000 feet – so we'll fly right over any storm we might encounter. "Besides," he continued, "we've got radar, GPS, and LORAN on board the Navajo. "Hey, we wouldn't even be getting into the airplane if there was any question. I've flown that route to Kulik so many times I could find it blindfolded!" he said.

Forty minutes later and half way to Kulik Lodge, the winds were careening off those mountains across Cook Inlet. Apparently a major storm system off the Aleutians was coming – headed our way.

But John Siegel looked as calm as ever up in the pilot's seat. My partner, John Staser, an Army major, just smiled, pretending not to notice any wind.

Thirteen minutes and forty-three seconds later I finally began to make out what appeared to be Nonvianuk Lake and Kulik Lodge off in the distance. A minute later I could also make out a very welcomed, long, wide Kulik gravel airstrip.

Flaring out over the lodge, John Siegel casually swung the twin around and plopped 'er down like he did this nearly every day, which he does. Pressing on the brakes, our pilot brought the Navajo to a sudden stop in a cloud of dust.

Kulik Lodge Manager, Bo Bennet, and head guide, Wayne Hansen were at the airstrip to meet us. Bo and Wayne had driven the mile from the lodge when John Siegel had radioed from the airplane, informing the lodge of our approach.

"You guys timed it just right!" Bo said as we hopped off the airplane, and dashed for the bushes. "Clients've been catching rainbows like crazy the past couple of weeks."

"Yeah– the rainbows are in –*and thick*– in very substantial numbers, indeed!" Wayne added.

I sneeked a peek over at John Staser and winked. "Told you!" I said. "I've just had this feeling of late!"

After introducing John Staser to Wayne and Bo I added, "Sounds like you guys need a couple of experienced fly-fishers to help you with too many fish!"

" Know any?" Wayne teased.

"No, come to think of it," I retorted, "but John, here, and I'll do our darndest to fill in until some *do* arrive!"

That brought the laugh we'd all been needing after a fairly hairy airplane ride. "I kinda figured we'd survive all along." John Siegel, our pilot teased.

Now that we were standing firmly on terra firma and Bo and Wayne had confirmed the rainbows were in –thick– the only question remaining was: Who'd outfish whom?

A visit to Kulik is always a fabulous lodge experience. "Angler's Paradise" they call it, and Angler's Paradise pretty much describes the area as well as anything I can think of. I sometimes try and imagine just what it would have been like to have been one of the original discoverers of that sacred Alaskan fishing spot several years ago; being one of the first to fly in to that country on floats and set 'er down and then venture off exploring and fishing a little. I had to admit, seldom in my travels across the state have I ever experienced superior scenery or better fishing than what exists at Kulik.

"Go ahead, scan the slopes around the area" Wayne Hansen had told me once. "After a while you'll begin to notice splotches on the hillsides that will begin to move, finally turning out to be caribou or bear, or possibly moose."

But for now there was both good news and bad news for my fishing companion and me. The good news was that we were at the very spot we wanted to be to experience some of Alaska's ultimate rainbow trout fishing. The bad news was that we'd have to wait until morning, because all of a sudden it was becoming late in the afternoon and the winds were suddenly increasing and the main lodge would be serving dinner in another hour and a half. Not enough time to grab our cabin, get suited up, make it over to a river, fish, and then return to the lodge in time for supper.

However, prime rib, prawns, fried chicken, baked red salmon, and Caesar's salad with fresh-baked rolls (with brownies for dessert) have a way of lessening the pain at such times. Consequently, my partner and I decided we'd slow down and savor all there is to be enjoyed at this premier Alaska fishing lodge.

It occurred to me how fortunate I had been over the years to experience all three of Katmailand's premier fishing lodges, Kulik, Grosvenor, and Brooks.

If I had to choose between 'em I'd be tempted to blurt out: Kulik, but on second thought, Grosvenor ranks right up there as one of my all-time favorites, too. And, Brooks *must* be ranked as high as any of 'em, both in the scenery department and in the fly-fishing. Believe me, choosing among those three is always a tough assiggnment.

But, on second thought, maybe Kulik's got a *slight* advantage...

At dinner, John Staser asked me about Grosvenor.

"Well, Grosvenor's a very intimate, 6-client lodge, situated in a very remote wilderness setting between two very pretty, wilderness lakes. "Naturally, Grosvenor has private showers and all the amenities, but it's at a beautiful, inaccessible place where world-class rivers flow nearby in both directionss. Right in the middle, right at Grosvenor Lodge, is one of the prettiest flows of all – a spot utterly perfect for rainbows, char, lake trout, and, of course, 'salmon in season.' "

"Grosvenor's especially unique," I continued, "in that only one guide and one cook/housekeeper are required to maintain the entire operation. The food at Grosvenor is terrific, of course, but, for me, the solitude, the beauty, and the built-in ambience of the place – along with the outstanding fishing found there really sets Grosvenor apart."

Feeling a tap on my shoulder, I turned, and there were Sonny Petersen, owner of Katmailand, Inc., and Jeff Moody, another of Kulik's experienced bush pilots. Naturally, it was great to see my old friends again, and I introduced them to John Staser.

I've had the privelege of flying with Jeff on several occasions; he's a bushpilot with thousands of hours of Alaska flying experience, flying the Bristol Bay and Katmai regions. Over the seasons I've even heard other lodge owners speak of their respect for Jeff Moody. That's quite a compliment, especially coming from other, competing lodges.

At dinner it occurred to me once again how enjoyable it is sharing fine cuisine and camaraderie at a first rate Alaska fishing lodge. Sure, it's always great to go out and experience great fishing, but to spend time at a first-class lodge, rubbing shoulders with the other guests – people from all over the globe – *that's* the stuff some of the purest fishing memories are made of. What it all boils down to is: romantic, adventerous types, people of all ages and social classes – have the opportunity to share their love for the outdoors and forget, for a few days at least, any troubles, struggles, deadlines, or red tape back at home.

Hey, it sure beats checking into a clinic.

Kulik Lodge is premier on it's own – not just because of the great fishing. Like few other lodges in Alaska that I'm aware of, Kulik is spectacular in the overall 'class' department. But that's not to call the place 'stuffy.' All things considered, Sonny and the other Kulik professionals have few peers when it comes to things called 'class' and service. Like somebody once told me, "Fishing at Kulik is tough work, but somebody's got to do it."

Next day meant fishin', and breakfast came at 6:00 a.m. sharp. Belgian Waffles, ham, bacon, sausage, French Toast, cinnamon toast, English Muffins, blueberry muffins, scrambled eggs, Eggs Benedict, fried eggs to order, crepes, omelettes, cantaloupe, grapes, grapefruit, raisins, oatmeal, fresh cream, hot coffee, orange juice, grapefruit juice, hot chocolate, wild raspberry drink, cranapple drink, cranberry drink, and ...

I was wondering if I was going to survive breakfast when head guide, Wayne Hansen stepped up and pointed to a blackboard they keep above the entrance to the kitchen. Among the items chalked on that board were the season's current top contenders for the biggest fish award (in fourteen or fifteen specie categories), along with guide / client pairings for the day.

"Looks like you two gentlemen are scheduled to go out fishing with me this morning for rainbows!" Wayne stated. What say after breakfast we climb into our neoprenes, hop in a floatplane, and go out and find ourselves a rainbow, or two?

I love it when guides talk like that.

Kulik is often described as being a dry fly-fisher's dream, and that's *not* a bad description. But since sockeyes were still present in the streams, this meant John and I would be nymphing single-egg patterns – *not* fishing dry flies. I could live with that.

During the next four hours, John and I caught and released approximately forty rainbows apiece – most in the 16 to 23 inch range.

When we finally stopped for lunch I asked John, "Did you see 'em ?" I said, "a brown bear sow and two cubs ambled by while you were fishing that one cutbank down by the bend!"

Those bears had added color to a morning of fly-fishing that will definitely go down in my book as one of the most amazing days spent fly-fishing a river in my life.

Forty rainbows in the 16 to 23-inch range in four hours?

Wayne hadn't fished, even though we tried to get him to. He merely wanted to watch us, provide us with egg patterns of any desired color, assist us with catch and release, and point out good riffles and runs. Every now and then Wayne would applaud the size of a fish.

He showed us how to rig our floating lines with a split shot and a single egg pattern that would drift underneath the salmon. A cast, a drift, and then *Wham!* Another spotted rainbow, seemingly appearing out of nowhere! Amazing.

John and I would have loved to stay and continue our fly-fishing, naturally, but the storm was building and moving in fast and the wind was on the increase. We had to decide whether to hop the Twin back to Anchorage that afternoon or risk spending four or five more days stranded away from our jobs in the city. It wasn't an easy decision, but...

After procastinating as long as we could, John and I decided to begin packing. Responsibility being the better part of romance and adventure we made the decision to tip our guide, pack our gear, and thank the fly-fishing gods for our brief – but amazing – fly-fishing experience at Kulik Lodge.

Halfway to Anchorage I glanced over at John who was staring out his window, still smiling.

"Do me a favor," I asked, "tell me *just one more time* how many rainbows each of us caught and released in a four hour period, will ya?"

Fly-Fishing Adventure #11
Showdown at Kenai Korral
with Bob Trout, Troutfitters

"Dan , there's a Mr. Bob Trout holding for you on line two," Kristy, our office assistant said.

When I picked up the telephone the voice at the other end was fuming:

"I don't believe this stuff you've been saying about outfishing me using a sinktip line!" Bob Trout said abruptly.

"I don't care *what* sinktip you might choose," he continued, "I'll be happy to wager anything you care to lose that I can outfish you using just a plain, old fashioned floating line and a simple strike indicator" he continued.

Bob's words weren't harsh, really– but they *did* seem to have a certain ring of seriousness to them. Besides, I realized, Mr. Trout was merely trying to get my adrenalin flowing, "spicing up the conversation" as they say, simply calling to inform me that he was finally ready to take me on.

"I'll tell you what, Bob" I countered. "If you want, I'll meet you down at the Alpine Inn motel in Cooper Landing this coming Friday at high noon, and I'll bring a couple of custom made sinktips that'll outfish any ol' floatin' nymphing outfit you've ever thought of stringin' on a fly rod."

"You're on," Bob announced in a cool, collected tone, "we'll go ahead and hold our own little shootout, but if it's okay with you, I'd like to invite Jodi, my sister in law to come join us. Jodi likes to fish, and when it comes right down to it, she's not such a bad little fisherperson, really."

"You go ahead and invite this Jodi lady or anyone else you'd like to watch me embarass you, Bob." I said. "Anything you want is okay by me. If you want to take your lumps in front of others then that's up to you, but you can count on me being down there at Troutfitters by noon on Friday – ready to fish!"

"Better be there right on time!" Bob said. "I've just got a feelin' we're going to get ourselves into some awfully big 'bows. I'll have the driftboat all ready to float. After all, the weather's been perfect, it's mid-September, and there're still enough salmon in the river to keep the 'bows and Dollies hangin' 'round. *Yeah!* It'll be good, all right. See you at high noon, Friday, Dan."

Well, I'll be! I thought, as I put down the receiver and shook my head. Bob Trout – *himself* – had called and challenged *me* to a fishing contest!

I had to admit, I liked Bob's style. But then, I'd liked Curt Trout's style a couple of weeks earlier, too. "These are guys with a good attitude about fly-fishing" I said to myself. But already I was busy thinking about how to outfish the veteran trophy fish catcher they call Mr. Bob Trout.

Oh, I'd be there on Friday, all right. Mr. Big Shot Bob Trout could count on that.

This was the very stuff my dreams are made of. Actually, it was a little like being an amateur golfer and having Tom Watson or some other great pro suddenly call up and ask for a shootout. I could just picture the conversation:

Be there at noon on Friday and bring your Ping Irons, Mr. hot shot. Me? I'll just stick to my ol' Rams.

I arrived at the Alpine Inn at approximately five minutes to twelve – almost two hours after leaving Anchorage. Not bad, considering the highway was still half torn up from all the road construction going on.

"Bob and Jodi are waiting for you down at the river, Dan" Rosemary Andres announced from behind the front counter. "I've put up lunches for the three of you...would you be kind enough to take them down to the driftboat?"

"This is getting to be a serious habit, Rosemary!" I said, recalling that she had supplied the lunches a couple of weeks earlier when I came down to fish with Curt."

I glanced at my watch. Already three minutes past noon. Already I was late. "I'd better be getting, Rosemary," I said. "Thanks again for the lunch! Real nice of you! Be sure and tell your husband, Richard, hi for me, okay?"

Bob was waiting down at Sportsman's Landing, where I'd met Curt Trout a couple of weeks earlier. Only difference was, Bob was over at the river with a rod in his hand – fishing. That's when Jodi strode up and introduced herself.

The first thing I noticed about Jody was the quality of her neoprenes and her fly vest. Both appeared to be of the very highest quality – something only a serious, experienced fly-fisher would purchase. Not only that, they appeared to be well-used. I could only hope Jodi wouldn't turn out to be some kind of fishin' wizard like her brother-in-law. Heck, I already knew I'd have my hands full just keeping up with Bob; the last thing I needed that afternoon was heavy competition from this Jodi lady.

Bob seemed cool and relaxed. The way he quietly and methodically arranged the gear for our drift reminded me of an artist, one systematically alligning his brushes for yet another masterpiece.

"You really think you're going to outfish me today don't you, Bob," I teased, handing over my rods and reels and the lunches Rosemary had prepared.

"No, I'm not really worried about anything 'cept enjoying ourselves today. Hope you and Jodi are *both* able to hook into some monster 'bows this afternoon – weather seems perfect for big fish today!"

The way Bob talked almost smacked of too much self-confidence. Maybe I'll just have to give this guy a fishin' lesson he won't soon forget, I thought. Just because he's fished the Kenai a thousand times and he's caught hundreds of trophy rainbows and knows the river like the back of his hand and knows what color egg-patterns to tie on at any given time...that didn't necessarily mean I was the underdog in this little competition...

Did it?

The Kenai appeared to be a little lower that it had been on my trip wi th Curt a couple of weeks earlier – more fishable – and lovely as ever, surrounded by dark Alaska spruce and those majestic mountains. Its mint-blue color always makes the Kenai unique among all other rivers.

And I had to admit, Jodi seemed like a very pleasant fishing partner; very personable and all, even if she did now have an expensive, state of the art 7-weight graphite fly rod in her hands. It wasn't long before we each had our gear arranged and ready to go. Jodi and I took our seats while Bob shoved off.

"Still going with a sinktip this afternoon?" Bob asked as he rowed, smiling directly at me. "You don't have to, you know. I'll be happy to let you fish any method you wish, as long as you stick to a fly rod, that is!"

"I'm going to show you just how to go about fishing big water this afternoon, Bob," I teased. "I'm going to give you a fishing lesson you won't soon forget!"

First stop was a lengthy gravel bank opposite a long, riffly run; good looking holding water that appeared to be a spot where hungry rainbows would be finning in two or three feet of water, just out of sight.

One of the things I liked about Bob Trout was that he wasn't the kind of guide who's always shouting instructions. Sure, he was more than happy to assist a client who asked for help, but he didn't try to force his tried-and-true methods on anyone.

Jodi was entirely competant enough to rely on her own instincts – and even though I hooked a nice four and a half pound rainbow on my sixth or seventh drift, I noticed through the corner of my eye that she had quickly hooked and released two Dollies, one of them appearing to be in the five-to six-pound range.

What followed was one of the best days of fishing I'd ever experienced – easily the finest fishing I'd ever experienced on the Kenai. "We slaughtered 'em that afternoon, didn't we, Dan?" was how Bob Trout described that afternoon a few months later, and Bob's descripion is as accurate and succinct as any I'd be able to come up with. We hooked and released rainbows and Dolly Varden trout all afternoon – absolutely premier fly-fishing any way you describe it.

One fish in particularly stands out in my memory: Even though I was fishing a G. Loomis 9 foot, 8-weight, IMX graphite fly rod, this particular rainbow had my rod bent nearly to the cork handle. I'd have hollered and asked Jodi or Bob to come up and assist me with the beauty, except for the fact that they were hooked up with fish at the same time.

What I remember most was that the fish didn't jump. At first I thought I'd hooked a Dolly, but the fish was a darter and a powerhouse of a bullier, not a jumper. Besides, Dollies usually twist and sound deep when hooked, usually heading for the deepest water they can find – while this fish had tried to use brute strength in breaking me off. Somehow I got the feeling this 'bow had been hooked a few times before and it had become educated itself on how to survive, but, of course, there was no way for me to confirm my theory. All I knew was that finally, after what must have been a ten or twelve minute battle, I eventually managed to pump that rainbow into the shallows before me, and there, all of a sudden, was one of the prettiest twelve-pounders I've ever taken. The only problem was that Bob and Jodi were busy battling their own fish – so in a senseless move, I attempted to merely keep my tired fish fifteen or twenty feet away on the hook, to give either Jodi or Bob time to come up and assist with a photo. Every so often I'd eye the spotted beauty again; this fish had a broad back and appeared to be about twenty-nine inches long: a trophy rainbow trout in anybody's book.

The kicker came only a minute or two later. Apparently, I was a little too sure of the anticipated photo and suddenly my trophy flipped off my hook. Presto – *gonzo!* Oh, well, no photo, but a good lesson to either grasp the fish gently and hold it in the currents, or reach down and unbutton it quickly, letting it swim back to its familiar haunts. The move I'd made had been dumb, a poor way to respect the trophy I'd hooked.

Live and learn, as they say. I'd didn't dare look up in case either Bob or Jodi had seen my error.

To say the least the three of us caught and released several mixed Dollies and rainbows that day. I don't remember, exactly, how many fish I caught, personally, but what I *do* remember, however, is that Jodi kept catching fish and catching fish and catching fish and...

Four hours later, when we'd nearly reached Jim's Landing, Bob queried me concerning the final tally. Jodi was busy playing another fish, so it gave Bob and me an opportunity to talk.

"Dan," Bob said, "I've already asked Jodi how many Dollies and rainbows she caught this afternoon and she told me that her number was something close to fifty. I know I hooked something like forty or forty-five, personally, so that makes about 100, and I'm just wondering if we met or broke the 150 mark?"

I confided in Bob that I'd taken maybe twenty-five, maybe thirty fish, all toll, but made him swear that he'd promise *never* to divulge that number to Jodi.

"No problem!" Bob exclaimed, "I understand what you're saying – completely. Don't let it bother you – Jodi outfishes me all the time! Don't worry, I know just how you feel."

What I didn't tell Bob was that I was getting to know that feeling all too well, myself. Just that season, alone, I'd already been outfished by several of the females I'd fished with. Nanci Morris over at Quinnat Landing Hotel in King Salmon has made a habit of doing it for years, now.

Another thing I didn't tell Bob was that I'd switched from a sinktip to a floating line and a couple of split shot early on during our drift. I'd have been thoroughly humiliated if I hadn't.

Being the consummate gentleman he is, Bob never said a word about the lesson he'd given me that afternoon – allowing me to retain a small portion of dignity, at least.

Back at the parking lot Jodi and Bob and I all shook hands. Not much was said because it was all too obvious the 'Showdown at Kenai Korral' had been very handily won by a lovely little lady named Jodi.

Fly-Fishing Adventure #12
"...Straight To Ugashik!"
from Quinnat Landing Hotel

"Nanci's probably going to join us; we'll find out if she has some free time once we get down to Quinnat," Doc said over the telephone. "All I know, is, I need to get out of town and go fishin' and I'm wondering if you'd like to come along and join Larry Smith and me, maybe meet us over at the 185 parked at Lake Hood next Saturday, say, around 8:00 a.m. ?"

I had to think about Doc's proposal. *For about twenty-four microseconds to be exact.*

"*Yes...ah...sure* I can make it, Doc! Want me to bring anything along? Need any food or fly rods or reels or any extra gear or anything?"

"Maybe grab a bucket of chicken – heck, we can survive off fried chicken all weekend long if we need to," he replied. "Don't know exactly how long we'll be gone, maybe bring a shotgun and a rifle with you, too – Larry said something about maybe stopping and huntin' caribou if we come across any out that way."

"A, sure, Doc, whatever," I said, "Need anything else? By the way, *Original* or *Extra Crispy?*"

"You'll probably want to bring a light change of clothes, 'cause we don't really know if we'll be out there for three days or five.

"Okay," I said, "I'll bring the fried chicken and meet you guys over at Lake Hood next Saturday morning!"

"By the way," Doc added before hanging up, "It's your turn to choose where we fly-fish this trip. If you'll remember, I was the one who got to choose last time we went out. This time, you do the choosing, okay? That's doctor's orders! See you Saturday morning, 8:00 sharp."

Dr. Joe Chandler didn't know it yet, but he was on his way to a place I'd wanted to fish for years called Ugashik Narrows.

Actually, the whole thing had started several years earlier when I first became acquainted with Dr. Chandler. Doc, as I call him, is one of the co-owners of Quinnat Landing Hotel, located on the banks of the Naknek River in King Salmon. I'd visited Quinnat five or six years earlier to do a fishing story with their head guide, Nanci Morris. During that trip I was introduced to Doc, who turned out to be a friend of a close friend of mine, and before I knew it I learned that Dr. Chandler loves to fish. He also loves to fly, especially, to some of Alaska's finest fishing spots. And, like me, Doc loves getting out of the city every once in a while.

"Not a bad sort of fellow! I remember thinking, my kind of guy, actually."

Then, a couple of years later, Doc invited me and a companion to join him in fly-fishing the American Creek and another stream located down by Lake Becharof that yielded 21-inch grayling and seven-pound char on nearly every other cast. *That* trip went down in my personal log as a trip definitely to be remembered. But even though the fishing had been superb, just spending time with Doc was all I could have asked for.

Doc's the consummate gentleman – simply a great guy to spend time with. He loves life, cares about people, enjoys flying, loves experiencing wild, scenic Alaska, and likes fishing a little, too.

Not necessarily in that order.

Could I make it over to Lake Hood by 8:00 next Saturday morning? Two guesses.

It took me a while to find it, but somehow I managed to rummage up the ol' 20-gauge shotgun (I hadn't even looked at the thing in five years). I finally remembered where I'd stored the ol' .06, too. Shooting caribou and hunting ptarmigan *wasn't* something I was particularly interested in, just then, but if Doc and Larry wanted to stop somewhere and get out and get some excercise and pop a few caps, more power to 'em. I'd either find a fishin' hole to pursue or fold down the seats and catch some shuteye.

The fly-fishing gods were obviously with us. Saturday turned out to be an absolutely picture perfect day to load up the floatplane and begin our trek across Cook Inlet over to the real Alaska, flying through Lake Clark Pass and points south.

Over Port Allsworth, Doc pulled back on the stick and nosed the Cessna to port, climbing up over the rugged mountains there, leveling-off at 4,500 feet, powering up over shimmering Tazimina Lake. From there we could see all the way over to Iliamna in one direction and all the way back to Lake Clark in the other.

"How about if we head directly for Quinnat Landing and King Salmon where we can grab some fuel and I can take care of a few little business matters before we hit the road again?" Doc asked. "Sound okay to you guys?"

Larry and I both nodded. Sounds just fine, Doc.

I'd enjoyed several great adventures fishing out of Quinnat Landing Hotel in earlier years. It's truly, "affordable luxury," located smack dab in the center of some of the best fishing and hunting areas in all Alaska. Visitors to Brooks Falls often choose Quinnat Landing as a base of operation. People of all ages and lifestyles can feel entirely comfortable at Quinnat – like I said in a magazine story, "...Quinnat's anything and everything a person could want, from filet mignons to hamburgers, from seafood a'la King to tuna, from hot fishing to photography - *just name it.*"

Some kind of convention was going on when Doc plopped the 185 down on the Naknek and taxiied over to Quinnat's ramp, so Doc and Larry and I left our gear in the airplane, freshened up in the bathroom, and joined the conventioneers upstairs in the restaurant for lunch.

Salisbury steak and stroganoff, together with fresh tossed salad and hot oven-baked dinner rolls would serve us just fine. The fried chicken would keep until we made it down to the riverbank.

"Looks like Nanci's got a couple of fly-fishing clients to take out this afternoon, so she won't be coming with us. By the way, Dan, I was just wondering...where're we headed, anyway? You never *did* say where you wanted to fish. *Fess up!*"

"Yeah!" Larry said, "I'd like to know where I'm going fishing this afternoon, too!"

"How about we fly straight to Ugashik, Doc?" I said matter of factly. "I've wanted to fish that place for I don't know how many years, now. Let's fly straight to Ugashik!"

"*Sure* you wouldn't rather go fish Blueberry Creek or Raspberry?" Doc asked. "After all, we could be there and be fishing in thirty minutes..."

"I'll be happy to go wherever you fellows want to," I responded, "but if I had my druthers, I'd really like to experience Ugashik if it's at all possible!"

"Tell you what," Doc said, "It's going on 1:15 pm now, so what do you say if we fly over and fish the American Creek this afternoon and evening for a few hours, and then fly back to Quinnat where we can get a good night's sleep? That way, we'll be ready to head to Ugashik first thing tomorrow morning. Anybody have any objections?"

Larry and I both agreed that it sounded like a fine plan.

"Okay, we'll go chase some rainbows tonight, and tomorrow we'll fly down to where the grayling grow to 22 inches, average, and where the lake trout and char are as long as your leg!

"Besides," Doc added, " Nanci mentioned something about Dr. David McQuire possibly getting back from his caribou hunting trip tonight, and something about Dr. Mike Cusack stopping over from *his* lodge, possibly joining us upstairs in the restaurant."

"Well, we'd better get ourselves back to Quinnat tonight, then," I said. "Sounds like there'll be some exciting stories to hear, to say the least."

Next thing I remember, Sunday was a bright, clear morning, with a slight wind drifting over the Naknek. That'll be okay, I thought; a little breeze would keep the bugs at bay and keep us cool as we fished.

A half hour later we were back in the floatplane and taking off upriver. Then, turning from the Naknek and banking south, we flew out across Whale Mountain, and then down the Alaska Peninsula, towards Lake Becharof. From my window in the Cessna, I could see for miles across the dotted tundra.

Below us, I knew, was prime caribou habitat. I'd hunted that area six or seven years earlier with my old friend Lew Marian. Little did I know then that that trip would be one of my final big game hunting efforts before fly-fishing would begin to occupy my full attentions. It's difficult to say, exactly, especially from an airplane traveling at 120 m.p.h., but I could almost swear I spotted the tiny, tundra lake Lew and I had camped on, a place that had formed an indelible memory in my mind.

Over to our port side was Becharof Lake. It looks different each time I view it, and this time it seemed larger than ever before.

Larry had the air charts out, navigating as we flew, although they weren't necessary, really, for off in the distance through squinted eyes we could begin to make out the reflection of what would turn out to be Upper Ugashik Lake.

Through the years I'd begun to see that Alaska's Ugashik Narrows (a strip of water approximately 250 yards long and perhaps only 75 yards wide between Upper and Lower Ugashik Lakes) occupies a special niche, unlike any other sacred water in the state. Sure, there are several other, similarly famous spots, like Lower Talarik Creek, and Brooks, and the Goodnews and (the list of other, great Alaska waters goes on), but somehow,

Ugashik Narrows always seemed to have a certain, almost reverent, cathedral-like quality about it whenever anyone mentioned its name.

Lee Wulff had spoken highly about Ugashik in his writings and audio tapes over the years. A couple of years ago Dewitt Daggett III had sent me a cassette tape of Lee Wulff reading an entire chapter he'd written, a chapter devoted solely to his fondness for Ugashik. I'd listened closely to that tape on many occasions, and I nearly had Lee's words mememorized. The more I listened, the more I knew that one day I wanted to visit Ugashik and experience its magic.

But my desire to go to Ugashik was not based upon wanting to catch big fish. Quite the contrary: I've always reasoned that big fish will come in due time.

No, I was more interested in simply experiencing Ugashik – for several years I'd wanted to set foot there and smell that place and wander around and catch a firsthand glimpse of it. If I happened to hook a big fish or two, I'd view that as icing on the cake. Most fly-fishers will know what I'm talking about when I say there's a certain, unmistakable "feel" to any fly-fishing water. And like the Henry's Fork or The Alagnak, or like Lower Talarik, I simply found myself wanting to taste of Ugashik's sweetness at least once in my life.

Before I knew it we were there. Suddenly Doc was pumping on the flap lever, lowering the flaps and easing down on the throttle, slowing the 185 down as we circled out over the Narrows. Then Doc pitched the Cessna down, down to the waters of Upper Ugashik Lake where he gently set the floatplane down, first on one float and then the other – then we taxied over to the spot just where the Narrows form. From there, we idled over to a beach where we hopped out and quickly tied the floatplane down. From there we'd begin our fishing on foot.

Upper Ugashik Lake was larger than I'd imagined. We hadn't really seen much of Lower Ugashik Lake, yet, but I suspected it was larger than I'd imagined, too.

Then it occurred to me; *we were the only ones there.* Here it was, a beautiful morning, and the winds had suddenly died down to almost nothing. The temperature was cool and pleasant; hardly a cloud in the sky. Besides that it was mid-September – the perfect time of year for fly-fishing – *and we had Ugashik Narrows all to ourselves!*

"Ugashik's a total catch and release grayling fishery these days," Doc said. "Seems somebody went and killed off too many of the grayling down here a couple of years ago, and so now it's strictly catch and release, but that shouldn't bother any of us, anyway."

I couldn't answer just then because I could hardly believe what my eyes were seeing. As Doc had been talking the huge, dark back of a grayling rolled in the currents directly in front of us. That fish *had* to have been at least 22 inches long. Not only that, it seemed to have a girth that would surely measure 14 or 15 inches.

"They're all over here like that," Larry remarked. "Look! There's a giant grayling, there, and another one, just over there. Heck, there are grayling surfacing around here everywhere!"

Larry was right; a school of monster grayling were surfacing all across the narrows. I was just about to tie on a dry fly when I remembered I'd forgotten to assemble my rod and reel.

"Here's an idea," Doc said. "What say we leave these grayling alone for an hour or so and move on down to the outlet, where the water spills into the lower lake? That way we can come back to good dry fly fishing on our way back to the airplane. I think there's some water down by the outlet you'll really appreciate."

Slowly, we worked our way downstream, working over tussocks and around beaver dams. There, the narrows widened. Where the channel makes a bend, several bright, fresh silver salmon could be seen, finning in the currents, resting lazily from their upstream migrations in the crystal flow.

"I think I'll try for some of these silvers," Doc said. "Dan, why don't you try that spot just downstream around the bend another hundred yards, or so. Last time I fished down that way I managed to hook into some very nice lake trout and char. . . I think you'll like it down there, Dan" he said.

I couldn't help but be impressed with the beauty of the place. Off to our left was a small peninsula where six or seven small cabins had been built, but farther downstream, around a bend, just where the narrows widen and shallow a bit was one of the prettiest pieces of water I'd ever laid eyes on.

I found myself trying to remember what it was Lee Wulff had said on his audio tape about experiencing Ugashik many years earlier. As I recalled he'd said something like, "*...it was a day to remember ... we felt its spell all day long as we fished...*"

Or something along those lines.

I had to admit, there *was* a certain kind of spell to Ugashik. I half expected to see a bear wander out from somewhere along there but we never did. If we had, it would only have added to the wild, lonely but lovely setting that makes Ugashik what it is – a place completely unique to Alaska.

I'd tied on a peach-colored, single egg 'glo-bug' as a "searcher" pattern. Then, wading out, nymphing as far down at the lower mouth and as far out into the flow as I could reach, I made a cast. I stripped out line and had allowed the fly drift and bob with the currents for a couple of minutes when I suddenly felt a tug at my line, just as I was beginning a retrieve for a second cast.

Suddenly my Hardy Marquise reel began screaming, and yards of backing began ripping off my spool. Larry and Doc had both fished their way down near by this time, so with an audience watching, it was all I could do to play this fish and not lose it. I soon realized this was no everyday fish.

By now, my 9 1/2-foot, 6-weight graphite fly rod was bent nearly to the grip and the spool showed that all but about thirty yards of my backing had disappeared in less than a minute.

"This *can't* be a grayling," I found myself saying, "..if it is, it's definitely close to the world's record. Man, ...it's *sure*... got ...some ...strength ...whatever it is!"

Slowly, carefully, I managed to gain back some of my backing a little at a time.

"It looks like you've hooked a fairly decent lake trout," Doc said, "take your time. What strength leader tippet are you using?"

"Thank heaven it's 2X," I answered, "something about 10 or 11 pounds breaking strength, I'd guess."

Fifteen minutes later, after giving and taking back line as gingerly as I could, carefully, very carefully, I started to gain line on the fish. For a while there my adversary had been 150 yards away from me and I thought there was little chance, but, by being patient and trying not to apply too much pressure to the rod tip, I finally managed to bring the fish to hand.

"It's a huge char!" Doc exclaimed.

"Yeah, it is...a *very* nice char," Larry added. It was then I noticed that I was breathing hard from the strain of the long battle.

"Get your camera out!" Doc ordered. "That's the biggest char I've seen in a very long time – come to think of it, I don't know if I've *ever* seen an arctic char any larger!"

I had to admit; the char was a trophy. The fly-fishing gods had definitely smiled on me that Sunday morning there at that lovely cathedral called Ugashik.

Quickly, I reached for my pocket sized camera and handed it to Doc. Then, turning my attentions back to the fish, I removed the barbless fly and revived the spotted beauty in the cool currents.

Suddenly Doc stepped up and announced, "There's no way you're letting this fish go. For all we know, you might have just caught the world's record Ugashik char! What size tippet did you say you were using?"

"Thanks anyway," I said, "But I'm not really into world's records, or state records, either, for that matter. Let's just get a fish mount created from the pictures we take. Taxidermists do that all the time these days, ya know. How about we just release this fish and get a fiberglass mount reproduced from a photo?"

191

"That's a fish of a lifetime," Larry cautioned. "If you release it, Dan, you'll always wish you'd kept it."

Across its deep green back and sides were the alternating, pink and orange spots so typical of mature char. Across its belly was a tangerine smear accented by a burnt-orange background, with brilliant white stripes on each of its lower fins.

Doc reached for his pocket tape and measured the char's length and girth. 32 1/2 inches in length and 18 3/4 in girth. Back at Quinnat, Doc would consult a chart that would confirm that my char had weighed at least eleven pounds or more.

I remember I was still breathing heavily as I held that beautiful char in those crystal, swirling currents.

We fished for another hour or so after that, but to be honest, I can't really say for certain just what I caught and what I didn't. I remember I hooked a few more grayling (just the average 3 1/2 or 4-pound Ugashik "commons," – fish in the 20 and 21 inch class) and another couple of pretty, orange-spotted char, but somehow my mind could only keep replaying the long-distance battle I'd experienced with that big, trophy fish I'd hooked on my first cast.

Doc proceeded to hook and play several fresh, bright silver salmon from the hole he'd discovered, while Larry stayed down near the mouth and fished with me, managing several big, chunky grayling, as well as three or four very fine char – all beautiful, trophy fish, each in the six or seven-pound range. Ironically, all of Larry's char looked small in comparison with the hulk I'd been lucky to hook.

Glancing at our watches we realized we'd been fishing the Narrows for approximately four hours and had had the place all to ourselves. Soon we heard the sound of an airplane approaching – a Beaver from a lodge over King Salmon way. After circling a couple of times, the pilot finally landed down near the lower mouth, where he taxied to the beach and cut the engine. A minute or so later five fishermen piled out.

Doc waded over. "Well, boys, we can continue our fishing," he said, "or we can fly back to Quinnat and still make it to Sunday brunch... whatever you prefer. Whadya think?"

"It sounds better than cold chicken, Doc," I teased, winking at Larry. "After all," I added, "it *would be* pretty difficult to top what we've already experienced this morning!"

"I agree," Larry added. "Why don't we pack 'er up and head back to King Salmon? We got what we came after. *Man*, it just doesn't get any better than this!"

Back at Quinnat, Doc consulted his fish chart. "If you'd been fishing a finer tippet, Dan" Doc said, "you just might have had yourself a world's record!"

"If I'd been using a finer tippet," I confessed, "I wouldn't have *landed* that fish, Doc!"

Since that day with Larry and Doc I've found myself dreaming of that morning spent fly-fishing at Ugashik at least a thousand times over. In my dream I'm standing out there in those swirling currents, just casting at that pretty spot down by the mouth where the narrows spill into the lower lake. Every once in a while I see myself with that big char on my line and I remember the impressive fight it gave, but more than anything, really, I see myself just casting, enjoying the cool flow of the water, completely entranced by the beauty of the place, unconcerned about whether I hooked many fish or not. It was enough just being out there, casting, and listening to the sounds of those currents.

Of course, in my dream Doc and Larry are out there fishing with me. And, like me, they're happy and smiling, just like we were on that first day, each of us just standing out there in that glassy flow, quietly casting our flies, each of us just savoring a little more of Ugashik's magic spell.

Fly-Fishing Adventure #13
KATMAI LODGE
After Season Finale' Grande'
Late September on the Alagnak

It was September 22 and Les Jacober's phone call came as a very welcomed surprise.

"Trey Combs and Ray Beadle are coming out to the lodge in a couple of days and Tony and I were wondering if you'd like to join 'em, maybe do a little dry fly fishing, maybe snap a picture or two for the new lodge brochure. You could hop the noon flight from Anchorage to King Salmon on Thursday, then catch the 207 shuttle over to the lodge that afternoon. *Sound good?*"

It was a loaded question. In the first place, Les knows I'm a sucker for anything that involves dry flies, especially when it also involves Alaska's famed Alagnak River. It'd be like me saying to my wife, "Honey, do you think we could run over to Nordstrom for an hour or two and do a little shopping and then stop at the furniture store and pick out a couple of new pieces?"

"Les," I responded, "neither rain, nor sleet, nor storm of night can keep me from my appointed duties. *Heck Yes* I'll be there!"

Of course I'd be there. After all, it *was* prime time for trophy rainbows and grayling. All I had to do was see that my business affairs in Anchorage were in order and clear the trip with my wife.

By the time Thursday came I was ready. As Les had suggested, I'd booked a seat on MarkAir's 737. Before I knew it, I was buckled in my seat and on my way to King Salmon.

That flight was a pretty one. Gazing out, I couldn't help notice the assorted fall colors scattered along the mountainsides and on the tundra below. Higher up, fresh snow had dusted the mountaintops – September's way of reminding me that this year's fly-fishing days were numbered.

When we landed at King Salmon the place looked half deserted. Somehow it wasn't the same town it is during the summer, especially during June and July. Then, everything's hurried and bustling – floatplanes are everywhere, horns are honking, babies are crying, and lodge vans are hustling visitors off in all directions.

But not this day. This was September 25. Tourist season had ended a couple of weeks earlier. Today, King Salmon, Alaska, seemed a rather loney place. The weather was grey and it was more than a bit gusty outside. Suddenly King Salmon was an entirely different place than it had been only a few weeks earlier.

Inside the air terminal, four of the five passenger windows had signs which read, Next Window Please.

Even though my flight over to the Alagnak would take only 20 minutes or so, the 207 wouldn't be leaving for almost another hour. Maybe I'd wander around town a bit, stretch my legs, "maybe get a little excercise," as Dad calls it.

I considered walking down Main Street, down toward Eddie's Fireplace Inn. Maybe I'd mosey down that way and grab a piece of cherry pie and down a diet Coke before my flight, but then I remembered; *this* was Thurday. Try as I may I couldn't remember if it was Eddie's or the other place up the street that featured *Wednesday Night RoundUp*. Either way, I decided, prudence probably *was* the better part of valor. Besides, it was barely 1:00 pm yet – who was to say what mood the waitresses might be in this early?

I thought about walking over to Quinnat, but figured *it* might pretty well be deserted, too. More than likely a convention was going on, and besides, Nanci Morris was probably off guiding fly-fishers upriver at Lake Camp, anyway. Vonnie and Tom might be on hand, but even if they were, they were probably stuck back in the office, steeped in paperwork.

Up in the opposite direction is King's Flying Service. I well remembered the caribou trip I'd made with them a few years earlier. After thinking about it, I decided maybe I'd wait until next season before I walked over and said 'hi' to John and Ellen.

Across the street and down a ways is the apartment house where whatshisname had lived. All things considered, he'd *seemed* like a fairly decent guy, really. *Somebody'd* said he'd made an adequate river guide, too, except for the fact that he'd been run out of town for taking deposits without showing up for his clients. Later I heard, *"Full Service Fishing"* is what he'd called it.

Back inside the terminal, Chimene, over at the MarkAir counter gave me one of her customary, big, friendly smiles – a nice thing to see on a lonely, grey, gusty day in King Salmon.

I'd just sat down and closed my eyes when Gary Evans, MarkAir's 207 pilot, brought me back to my senses.

"Ready to fly over to Tony's?" Gary asked. "Airplane's all warmed up. I'm ready to go whenever you are – we'll be haulin' over a load of lumber, but other than that it's just you and me."

That flight was spectacular. Gary took the Cessna to only 400 feet or so – way below ceiling – so visibility seemed endless.

Three shades of yellow, along with assorted ochres, greens and various oranges and reds dotted the rolling, pock-marked tundra below. I saw a couple of moose, but no caribou surprisingly – and not a single bear. I leaned over to the pilot and said, *"Sure wish Dad were here to see this."*

For fly rods for this trip, I'd decided on my ol' reliable, my 9 1/2 foot, G. Loomis 6-weight IMX, along with a 9-foot, 8-weight Loomis GL3. My thinking was: I could still throw tiny bugs with the 6-weight, even though the fishing might not be quite as enjoyable as maybe using a four or a five. On the other hand, if the water was high and we found ourselves throwing heavy leeches and buggers on Teeny T-200s and possibly T-300 shooting heads, the 8-weight would supply me the power I'd need.

For a set of reels (to be safe, I always try to carry a matched pair) I'd selected a couple of Hardy Marquise #6s. Over the years I've acquired several extra spools (already wound and ready to go) for this reel size, everything from 5-weight through 8-weight, from various floaters to a full array of sinktip lines.

The scenery just kept getting better as we flew, and before long Gary and I could see the lodge approaching off in the distance. Tony Sarp's KATMAI LODGE makes for an impressive sight from the air. The place consists of something like 28 separate buildings: large buildings, small buildings, guest quarters, a sauna building, a lodge post office, several guides' quarters, the main dining hall, a guest lounge, and four or five new 2-story units. It's all right there, just on the banks of the wild, pretty Alagnak. Visitors can travel to the lodge either by floatplane or simply land on wheels at the lodge's long, dirt strip.

Tony's head guide, Tom Haugen, met us as we landed, and it didn't take long to learn that Tony, Trey, and Ray were already out fishing upstream in the Braids. I'd just waived goodbye to Gary and had reached for my bag and rod tubes when Murray Armstrong, another lodge client, approached and introduced himself, explaining that he'd arrived earlier that morning.

"What say we get suited-up, grab our fly rods, hop in a boat and motor upstream and see if we can locate Tony and the others?" Tom asked. "I've got a radio on board, so we can call 'em if we need to, but we can stop and fish at selected places along the way. Sound good?"

"I can be ready and be down at the boat in ten minutes!" Murray and I said almost in unison.

Twenty minutes later we pulled up behind an island in the braids. "Nice looking confluence right up there, just around that corner," Tom pointed. "What say we get out here, string 'em up and go fish that spot?"

"Couldn't agree more, Tom," we said. Two minutes later we'd waded out waist high. Because of big water, I elected to go with the 8-weight. I'd be throwing a Teeny T-200 sinktip line.

Tom handed me a fly to try. "It's called a *Sarp's Perfect*," he said. "A friend of Tony's designed it for him a couple of years ago – over the seasons we've learned it catches fish like crazy!"

I'd never fished one quite like it, but I had to admit, Sarp's Perfect did look like it'd catch fish. Actually, it appeared to be but a slightly fancier version of white Egg-Zonker, tied on about a size-4 hook. It's basically a white attractor pattern, with a flame-colored egg tied in at the head.

"*Thanks!* I'll give it a try." I said.

With the confluence directly in front of me, I could cast my fly line slightly to either side of the break and end up with a drift to my left *or* to the right. The T-200 felt about right, possibly a tad light, but on my second drift, allowing my fly to dredge deep in the currents, I suddenly felt a jolt and realized a good size rainbow had climbed aboard.

'Sarp's Perfect' had definitely fooled this rainbow, that much was obvious. But for some reason, this fish didn't jump. Instead, it darted all around the place like a house afire. One minute I'd be fighting the fish to the left, the next I'd be fighting to my right. It was the first fish I'd hooked using the new, Loomis, GL3 graphite material, and I found myself very pleased with the rod's performance.

When I managed to bring the 'bow to hand I realized I'd hooked a buck – or male fish. That made sense. Males don't jump as frequently as females do, for some reason, but they *do* tend to power-down harder, fight deeper, usually offering a little more resistance and a somewhat longer battle.

When I managed to bring the fish to hand, I noticed this rainbow's back and fins were profusely dotted with black spots, and it's sides and face plate were a deep, crimson red. Definitely a river fish, it was a nice, 26-incher, approximately a 7 pounder I guessed, a beauty of a rainbow that I'd be happy to hook any time – any day of the week.

Glancing downstream a ways, I could see that Murray had hooked a fish, too. That was about the time I stopped to realize, once again, how happy I was to be standing at that very spot at that very minute. There I was, I thought, fly-fishing one of the rivers in Alaska that is dearest to me, the time of year was perfect, the weather was superb, and we were out there fly-fishing with one of Alaska's most experienced guides. To top everything off, I'd just hooked a 7-pound rainbow on my first cast.

I wondered: 'What is it about fly-fishing, standing out in the middle of a clear, glistening river that tends to bring out so much emotion in a fly-fisher?' There's *something* magical about it, that much is for certain.

A second later, Tom let out a whoop. His rod was doubled way over, too.

It didn't take long to see that Tom had hooked a bright, hefty coho, a powerhouse of a silver salmon that wasted no time putting on an aerial display of powerful flips and tail dances, sending a showery spray across the current with each thrashing leap.

If I'd had my wits about me, I'd have pulled out my camera and snapped a photo of Tom fighting that silver, but I guess I was so taken in by the action I merely stood there and watched.

"Time's slipping by," Tom said after he'd released his salmon. "Maybe we should try to find Tony and the others."

It was 3:30 p.m. The days in Alaska were getting shorter. I figured the sun would set sometime around 6:30.

Suddenly, around a bend came Tony's jet boat, a riverboat that's very easy to identify.

Tony was standing at the helm, and I could tell by his smile that he was out having fun after a long season of fulfilling the responsibilities of operating one of Alaska's premier fishing lodges.

Tony pulled the boat to shore and one of the passengers hopped out and hurried over to where I was standing.

"Dan, I'm Trey Combs...pleased to meet you!" the man said. Almost before I could get a word out, another, taller man approached. "Dan, I'd like you to meet Ray Beadle" Trey said.

Naturally, it was a thrill meeting both of these gentlemen. Both are fly-fishing legends in their own rights, I knew, but I found myself more than a little astonished at how personable both of them seemed.

I'd heard Ray Beadle's name on various occasions, and my inclination to associate him with saltwater fly-fishing turned out to be correct.

Trey, on the other hand, is probably best known for his expertise on steelheads. I'd probably read his book, 'Steelhead Fly-Fishing and Flies' (Amato Publications, ©1976) at least a dozen times over the years.

Heck, I'd spent scores of hours *studying* the thing.

Since then, of course, Trey Combs has published his consummate treatise on steelheads, *Steelhead Fly Fishing* (Lyons & Burford, 1991), a book that is considered *the* source not only of information on steelies, but is a true masterpiece among fly-fishing books. "A book I'd be proud to keep on the front room coffee table" is how I described it to my wife.

One thing was very obvious, however: Trey Combs and Ray Beadle were as excited as I to be at The Alagnak.

The amazing part was, here it was, seeming just like old home week, and I'd only just met these guys. It was exciting, too; *heck*, you could *feel* the excitement in the air. Tony Sarp probably put it best when he walked over and officially introduced me to Murray Armstrong. "It doesn't get any better than this, fellas!"

Even though I'd suddenly found myself surrounded by several world class anglers, it occurred to methat these guys were not much different from other fly-fishers. We were all just out there to have a good time on one of Alaska's ultimate rivers. Everybody was jus' regular folk, jus' regular fly-fishers, everybody out enjoyin' themselves. Everybody having a good time, *fish or no fish*. I remember thinking, *This* is the way fly-fishing always ought to be.

But there *were* fish. Plenty of fish. *Rainbow* fish.

Since each of us was already rigged with a sinktip, the grayling dry fly fishing would have to wait for another evening. Not enough time tonight to restring to floaters and tie on dries. There *was* time for a little rainbow fishing, however.

At Tony's request, head guide, Tom Haugen led both boats down to one of his favorite holes.

When we arrived, two large bull moose, both carrying massive, 65-inch antlers, crossed the river just downsteam from us. That was when I remembered; *this* was September – September is when moose rut.

Bald eagles circled overhead and were perched above us in the trees in the fading light as we assumed our positions and began our casting. My, but that river was pretty at that hour. Wild ducks and geese skimmed the river, whizzing by just over our heads. That brown log drifting down the river, wasn't a log at all, but a beaver trying to make us believe otherwise. We didn't see Mr. Brownie that evening, but we *did* see where he'd stepped down to the riverbank just before we'd arrived.

Tony waded out farther and deeper than any of us, sometimes to the point where I was surprised that he wasn't swept away by the currents. Trey, on the other hand, picked distant points, out where seams and confluences joined. Ray Beadle and I tried to select more moderate flows, places hungry rainbows might lie in wait, eager to intercept either insects or loose, drifting salmon eggs. Murray seemed to like the deep, big runs, probably a habit he'd acquired from fishing steelhead over so many years.

I can't recall for certain who caught the most fish, but it doesn't matter, and it certainly wasn't me. Truth of the matter is, we *all* caught fish, that much I do recall. What I remember about that evening's fishing more than anything was the fun and the laughs we shared together. We were like a bunch of schoolboys out havin' a good time. Tony Sarp, especially. Tony was out there really enjoyin himself, "I've waited all year to fish," he said, "and by golly, I'm going to *fish* for a few days!"

Eventually it grew too dark to fish, so we clipped our flies and disassembled our rods and decided to beeline it the 20 or so miles downstream back to the lodge.

Bev and Annie had volunteered to cook-up some of their famous steaks on the grill that evening, so by the time we pulled up at the dock the aroma of juicy tenderloins sizzling over the barbeque beckoned us to shed our neoprenes and get over to the dining hall pronto.

Naturally, that evening was filled with stories of fly-fishing, but more stories of saltwater fly-fishing were told than stories of steelhead and of Alaska's rainbows and king salmon.

Murray and I just sat back and listened intently while Tony, Trey, and Ray all extolled tales of days spent fly-fishing at sea for exotic species like sailfish and wahoo, barracuda and permit, trevally and bonefish.

What's a trevally? I'd teased Murray.

It was all fascinating stuff, sitting there, listening, taking it all in. I found myself astonished at the number of saltwater species these guys had succesfully landed on fly rods over the years.

And here I thought Trey Combs only fished for steelhead!

Every once in a while Murray and I would glance over at each other and shake our heads.

Someday. *Maybe.*

Next morning came all too quickly, and it was cold. Not exactly ice on the river, but darn close.

Skies were clearer than the day before, so it was noon by the time we felt any warmth from the sun. Until then we'd kept warm by casting, powering T-200s and 300s, usually with *Sarp's Perfect* tied on at the ends of our leaders.

Ray Johnson was our guide on the river that day. I'd come to know Ray earlier that season, back in June, and I knew Ray Johnson to be one of the best fishing guides I'd ever had the pleasure to fish with. Ray's a total gentleman, a very knowledgable fly-fisher, and what's more, like Tom Haugen, Ray's a lot of fun to be around. *What more is there?*

We all knew the grand finale was still to come. Heck, we could *feel* it coming. Of course, we didn't know exactly what it'd be, per se, or to whom it would happen, but it was just too pretty out there on that river that September afternoon for *something* not to happen. Conditions were simply too perfect; a gentle breeze, the water temperature was warming, the outside temperature was now merely cool, comfortable...

Who would carry the lucky rod?

Murray Armstrong? Ray Beadle?

Then it happened. It happened all of a sudden at around 6:00 in the evening at a glassy, silky, fairly deep flow just below an island in the Braids.

We were all just standing there, casting in waist deep water, casting and laughing at Tony's antics, throwing floaters with long leaders attached with small gnats and the like tied on, fishing to a pretty decent grayling rise where small 'bows would show themselves every once in a while and manage to get hooked every now and then. We were all catching fish, catching fish on every other, or every third cast it seemed.

The grayling were plentiful. And fun. And large.

We'd all hooked several of them when Tony Sarp hollered that his 3-weight graphite rod was bent to the cork.

"Feels like a *big* fish, boys..." Tony muttered, real serious-like.

Naturally, we all teased him, *"Sure, Tony, probably just another 3-pound grayling!"* Then we'd continue with our casting.

But Murray Armstrong knows Tony Sarp well, and after a minute I noticed that Murray had quit casting and was watching intently as Tony battled his fish. That was about the time I noticed Tony's rod *was* bent. Just maybe Tony *did* have a big fish on! Looking around again, I could see that Tony's rod was *really* bent.

That was about the time Trey and Ray quit fishing, too. Everybody moved over and started watching Tony Sarp play his fish.

"I'm telling you guys...it's BIG... this is a big fish, ... boys," Tony kept saying as he pumped and reeled, pumped and reeled. "It's big, trust me....and it's....*strong*...." Every once in a while he'd let out a little laugh. But the more we watched, the more we could see the seriousness build in Tony's face.

I don't know how, but somehow that little G. Loomis 3-weight fly rod of Tony's stayed together. And, somehow, don't ask me how, Tony's tippet continued to hold...

Tony was fishing a dark, size 14 Elk Hair Caddis, and somehow the 11-pound rainbow Tony hooked had finally succumbed to temptation and had surfaced and gulped the fly and had turned and tucked the fly neatly in the corner of its upper lip. Somehow, don't ask me how, Tony managed to hold on to his fish, and now, almost a half-hour later, Tony was ready to land himself an 11-pound Alaska rainbow trophy.

On a 3-weight, 7 1/2 foot, 1 and 1/2 oz. fly rod!

Trey and I glanced at each other, then quickly handed our rods over to the other guys and jumped in to assist Tony with his spotted trophy. We both reached for the fish and our pocket cameras at the same time and began snapping photos.

"Just *look* at this fish, boys!," Tony kept saying. "Waahooooo!!...*Jus'* look at it, fellas! Sure wish my brother, Buddy, was here to see this beauty!"

Tony was right; none of us could believe either the size *or* the beauty of Tony's huge, spotted rainbow.

Taken on a size 14 dry fly on a 3-weight fly rod?

I moved over and held the huge rainbow while Trey snapped more closeups.

"*You* release him, fellas," Tony said finally. "I just want to stand back and admire the sight...I just want to watch it swim away...*prettiest rainbow* I've caught in a long, long time, fellas!"

With that, looking to see that Tony was ready, I released my grip. With one flick of it's tail the huge rainbow disappeared.

Together, Tony and Trey and the rest of us let out a whoop and a holler that could have been heard a mile away, probably scaring those bull moose we'd seen earlier.

"If you'll let me, maybe I'll use this rainbow on the cover of my next book, Tony!" I voiced.

Needless to say, the six of us were in pretty rare form that evening – Tony saw to that – so we figured it was probably time to call it a day and pack 'er up and head back to the lodge. Besides, Tony was buyin' tonight. After all, he was the lucky so-and-so who'd gone and hooked the *big* fish, even though he was host to the whole affair.

Showoff.

To be honest, I don't really remember much after that. That rainbow of Tony's was topped only by the camaraderie and the laughs and the stories that were told at dinner that evening. Bev and Anne had worked up a delectable salmon and steak combo dish including fresh-baked rolls and a garden fresh salad with oodles of blue cheese dressing – typical of Katmai Lodge's constant menu of great food.

If I remember right, this was the evening that Murray and Tony talked of huge king salmon they'd taken on fly rods downstream on the Alagnak, and spoke of steelhead trout they'd taken in other years over on the Skeena and other famed steelhead waters.

Afterwards, Trey and Ray got to telling about saltwater fish and shock tippets and saltwater rigs and...

"Bimini Twists? What's that, Murray?" I teased.

The following morning and I was down at the dock waving goodbye to Trey and Ray as Tom Haugen warmed up the engine for what Trey described as 'just one more day's' rainbow fly-fishing before freeze up."

It was cold, I remember. All three of those guys had drawn up their hoods, and all three wore gloves, along with big smiles on their faces. Trey muttered something about going back up, fishing the braids for a twelve pounder, something bigger than Tony's huge rainbow.

Me? I was on my way back to Anchorage, back to the wonderful world of pressure and deadlines. Gary'd be along in MarkAir's Cessna 207 presenty, and together we'd fly over to King Salmon. During the flight I'd look to see if more snow had fallen on the mountaintops.

But not before I thanked Tony Sarp for one of the greatest fly-fishing adventures of my life.

Fly-Fishing Adventure # 14
Skunked, On The Kenai ?
Drifting from the Kenai Kadillac

Suddenly it was October 5 and the days were getting shorter in Alaska. It wasn't all that evident at first, but night *was* falling sooner and the temperature was dropping noticably. But at least snow hadn't fallen.

Yet.

Nobody wanted to admit it, but summer was fading – and fast.

As I recall, it was a Tuesday evening during David Letterman when Tom Coomer called to inform me of his new investment – a portable floating device – something between a raft and a catamaran – a thing they call a "cataraft."

"You gotta see this thing, it's a beauty!" Tom said. "I've been toying with the idea of getting one for over a year now. Last weekend I finally broke down and bought one. Had to, really; the deal was just too good to pass up."

"The guy at the raft shop even knocked an extra hundred bucks off the sale price," Tom continued, "and to make the deal impossible to refuse, he even threw in a free repair kit when I stewed for a minute. Wanna try it out with me on the Kenai?"

I had to admit, Tom's offer was attractive. Besides, I wasn't close to putting the rods and reels away – not just yet, anyway.

Not only that, I'd never drifted from one of the new catarafts before. And with Tom driving, maybe I'd finally get a chance to outfish him for a change.

Hmmm...

"Ah...yes...sure, Tom, I'd be pleased to venture down to the Kenai with you and try out your new toy. Wanna take two vehicles, or should we just go in one? We can take my Blazer if you'd like."

"Let's just take my pickup." Tom said. "I've already got the raft deflated and loaded – the metal frame is all that's still assembled. I strapped that to the top of the pickup. The pontoons are folded in the back of the truck. I've even have an electric pump, so we can blow it up and assemble the thing in less than a half-hour once we get down there. I've still have a couple more days of vacation, so maybe we could think about slipping away on Friday. How does that sound to you?"

"Friday sounds great, actually." I said. "Hope this weather holds. What say I meet you Friday morning at your place at 5:30 – that way we can drive down to the river, inflate the pontoons, assemble the raft, and be out drifting by 8:30 or so. Sound okay?"

"See you at 5:30 Friday," Tom said.

This was great! I thought. Just what I'd needed – at least one more day of fly-fishing for the season – another chance to reconcile with the reality of the coming of the end.

For me, fly-fishing has always been one of the more enjoyable ways to escape the responsibilities of everyday life. I definitely was looking forward to squeezing in another fly-fishing venture before 4th quarter officially set in and advertising quickly took over my life once again.

Besides, with Tom at the helm, maybe I'd finally have a chance to outfish him for a change...

I can't say I remember much about the drive down to the Kenai. Being a 'night owl,' 5:30 a.m. comes awfully early in my book. We *did* wind up taking two vehicles, however. Tom said something about having to get back to Anchorage early that evening – free tickets to the opera or something. Consequently, I decided to just follow Tom down. That way maybe I could get a little longer feel of the river before finally facing another long Alaska winter.

Then it occurred to me: This wouldn't be the last fly-fishing excursion of the year! *No!* Considering that I'd be looking advertising dead in the face for the next seven months, this trip, and a few more just like it, would be both medicinally and emotionally therapeutic. I'd have to remember to explain that to my wife when the time came.

Besides, Eli had told me he'd be down fishing the Kenai about then, too. Maybe Tom and I'd bump into him while we were there.

After about a two hour drive Tom and I pulled up at Sportsman's Landing. I'd almost managed to pull my neoprenes up and was halfway finished tying my stream boots when Tom announced, "Okay, she's ready – let's do it! Let's make the maiden voyage!"

"Why don't you christen her, "Miss T," after your significant other?" I ventured.

"Yeah, good idea" Tom said wryly. "Maybe we could call it Misty...the Kenai Kadillac! Okay, enough foolin' around. Hop on – let's go see if we can catch us a fish or two."

I had to admit, Tom's new cataraft was great to ride on; kind of a "Kenai Limo" the way I saw it.

My seat was on the right front pontoon, which gave me a great view of the river. It even had a seat belt, and the seat swiveled, so I could cast around in all directions.

"This is really neat, Tom – thanks a lot for buying it!" I teased him.

Now it was time to tie on a fly. Real careful-like, looking around to make sure Tom wasn't watching, I reached in my fly box and picked out a nice little "electric glo-bug," a pretty little pink offering; with a glint of pearlescent "flashabou" tied in to give it "added attractivness."

I couldn't wait to hook a fish.

I could just imagine the look of frustration on Tom's face when I landed my first, really big rainbow! Finally, justice would be served, I thought. Today might just be the day I'd waited for for a long, long time.

In fact, I'd gone to special pains to outfish Tom. For one thing, I'd selected an 8-weight fly rod, just in case I happened to hook one or two of those world famous, monster Kenai rainbows in the ten, twelve, or even fifteen pound class. And, just to make *sure*, I'd tied on a 12-pound leader tippet section – some of that new, fancy stuff from Maxima called Ultragreen™ – almost

214

guaranteeing me a couple of giant fish. I kinda felt bad, but Tom just didn't have a chance.

Not today, at least.

Surprisingly, an hour later, when we pulled over just behind the big rock where the two wide flows of mint blue currents seperate, neither of us had hooked a fish.

Yet.

There had to be a reason, I thought.

But then, maybe I wasn't quite awake yet. After all, it wasn't even 10:00 a.m. Quite possibly my touch at this early hour just wasn't quite "there" yet.

No problem. "We'll get 'em, Tom."

Nothing to worry about. It was early yet. After all, Bob and Curt Trout had shown me how to fish the Kenai – blindfolded, almost. Child's play, really. Just a matter of going through the paces, I reassured myself.

"We'll get 'em, Tom. By the way, if you need me to help spell you with the driving, don't hesitate to ask, okay?"

An hour later we pulled into a backwater slough, a wide, fairly silty spot where we could pull over and hop off and stretch our legs a bit, maybe eat a sandwich or two. The place reeked of dead, rotten salmon, but against such a magnificent setting as that one, it didn't smell *that* bad, mind you.

"T" helped me put a few lunch items together...maybe we should take a minute and have lunch right here," Tom said. "I'll open up the cooler – just grab whatever you like, Dan."

Tom was right. Terese had spared no effort providing a fine lunch for this little drift of ours. Heck, I'd fished out of lodges that hadn't provided food this good. Maybe I'd go easier on Tom after lunch, I thought – at least in the fish catching department. "Please pass the Virginia cured ham and maybe just a little more provolone, perhaps the Dijon mustard and possibly another sweet pickle and how about just one more Diet Coke to wash down these Pepperidge Farm soft baked, soft and chewy, extra large chocolate chunk cookies, wouldya, Tom?"

Darn, but the river was pretty that day. Those sandwiches tasted extra delicious against that awesome Kenai scenery, regardless of the rotten salmon stench. The Kenai was mint blue that day, set against dark green Alaska spruce trees, with puffs of white, fluffy, Roy Rogers clouds hanging in a powder blue sky.

"Man, it just doesn't get any prettier than this Kenai River country, does it, Tom?" I said. "Are all the sandwiches gone?"

"Yeah, it's pretty, all right," Tom said, "..but all I've caught is that *one* fish so far and I'm startin' to wonder what it is I'm doin' wrong," he replied.

"What fish...er, ah...how many fish did you say you've caught?" I asked.

"Just that one rainbow." he repled, "You know, up there a ways by the big riffle while you were busy fishing that deep hole, just where the left channel spills over that big, rusty-colored boulder over on the left."

"Oh, yeah, *that* fish. I didn't see you catch it...guess I was too busy working that deep hole, like you said!

216

"Good for you, Tom. *Good for you*," I added. "Hey, got any more of them rippled potato chips? They're really tasty – didn't you think they made quite a nice addition to the meal?"

Right about then it occurred to me that we were almost half finished drifting the Upper Kenai and I hadn't even had a strike. To make matters worse, Tommy Boy had – methodically – already taken a fish, and here he was complaining that the fishing was poor.

Now it was time to really get serious. Secretly I reached for a big, black and brown woolly bugger and tied it on to my leader tippet.

"Tom, if you'd like to sit up front and let me drive, I'll be more than happy to take the helm," I reminded him.

"Nah, I'm doing fine, even though I don't get to fish quite as much sitting back here," Tom said. "You just stay up front there and enjoy the drift – besides, you'll be able to reach more water from up there."

As quickly as possible, I added a fluorescent yellow strike indicator to the end of my leader. For the next hour I watched it like a hawk, but, alas, no twitches, not even a slight wobble. Either there were few fish or I needed to see an optimologist. A.S.A.P. It occurred to me maybe I was jinxed that day.

Intently, I'd cast to the left, to the right, over by bushes, in close, nearer the raft – nothing!

Finally, out of pure frustration but still retaining my "cool," I retrieved my floating fly line and slipped on a spare spool containing a Teeny T-200 sinktip line.

This'll get 'em, I remember thinking. I'll just dredge the bottom while we drift and I'll begin picking up rainbows and Dollies one after another. Besides, it's becoming late afternoon, and late afternoon is always when fish begin to bite!

By now we'd passed the "Big Island Hole," "The Washingmachine Hole," and the "Whirlpool Hole," and still nothing. Suddenly, things were beginning to get tense. Then, just where a small channel leaves the main river, Tom pulled us over.

Jumping out, I secured the raft and Tom and I hoisted it up on to the beach. We'd leave it there for a half-hour or so while we waded down and fished the little outlet.

Usually, red (sockeye), silver, or pink salmon could be found at that spot – but not this day, not October 7. In fact, try as I might, I could not spot a single fish. Heck, I couldn't buy a fish. And I would have, believe me.

We were just working our way back to the raft when Tom hollered. Turning back, I saw that Tom had hooked another fish.

"Way to go, Tom!" I shouted.

Drats. Other than those rotten salmon back where we ate lunch, I still hadn't seen a fish – dead or alive!

Well, I could take you through the whole ugly scenario, but in the end, after we'd pulled into the final take-out spot, Jim's Landing, I had to admit, I'd been skunked.

Maybe I'd tried too hard, or maybe the fly-fishing gods had figured I'd already caught my allotment of fish that year – I'm not certain.

That was about the time I looked over on the beach and spotted Eli. "Eeeeliiiii," I shouted. "Have any luck this morning? When'd ya get down here?"

"Slept in the back of the pickup last night," Eli said. "Cold as heck, didn't wake soon enough, though, didn't get out fishin' 'til 'bout 6:00. Only picked up six, no, maybe seven or eight I think it was, mixed Dollies and small 'bows. How'd *you* do?"

"Man it's pretty down here right now isn't it?" I said. "Don't you think, Eli ? I'll bet the boys back in Anchorage were sure wishing they were down here today, what with all this nice weather and all...river's as mint-blue as I've ever seen it, and these mountain backdrops are sensational – man, what a great day for a drift. What'ya think of Tom's new Kenai Kadillac?"

Eli helped Tom and me deflate and disassemble Tom's cataraft, helped us lift the metal frame up on the pickup where it'd get strapped down once again, ready for the drive back to Anchorage.

"I've got that opera thing tonight" Tom remembered. "I'd best be hittin' the road back to town."

Naturally, I thanked Tom for the great day we'd shared together, the good companionship, and, of course, the great drift on his nice, new raft, including the tasty lunch Terese had supplied. I'd meant to congratulate Tom on his two fish but somehow it slipped my mind.

"Eli," I said, "what say we drive up to Summit Lake Lodge and have ourselves a piece of cherry pie? I don't know about you, but I'm not quite ready to call it quits for the season just yet."

Eli didn't answer, only nodded his head and stared down at the ground, looking rather sad for a change. I could tell by his expression that Eli had also realized that this was *it* – the final fly-fishing outing of the year – never an easy thing for any dyed-in-the-wool fly-fisher to swallow, not when it comes right down to it. "How about I follow you up to Summit Lodge?" I asked.

Pie was good as always but there wasn't a lot of talk as we sat there, gazing out the large bay window, just peering out across the empty lake. Seems a big, ominous storm had chosen that hour to gather. A few minutes later, right on schedule, snowflakes began falling, settling on the windowpane. Suddenly, another long Alaska winter had begun.

That's when it occurred to me that I'd forgotten to mention something to my friend.

"Eli," I said, "I've been doing some thinking. Trey Combs has invited me to bring a partner and join him down at Ascension Bay on the Yucatan Peninsula this coming February for bonefish, permit, barracuda, snook, and baby tarpon – all on the fly. Think you might want to join me and tag along?"

There was a long pause as I watched Eli's eyes grow to the size of dinner plates, a smile beginning at the corners of his mouth.

"I got an idea," Eli said. "Why don't we order a double cheeseburger and large fries for each of us? After all, we're not in any particular hurry, are we? And, besides, I think I'm starting to get my appetite back. Not only that, *I'm buyin'!*"

Eventually I waived goodbye to Eli and watched him drive away. Snow was still painting the tops of those steep Kenai mountains as I started my vehicle and made the drive up over Turnagain Pass and down to Hope, slowly working my way back down to sea level. It was as if nature was confirming that the end of fly-fishing season had finally arrived – and that the beginning of winter was officially upon us.

During my drive back to Anchorage it occurred to me once again how lucky I am to be a fly-fisher, especially one who lives in Alaska, the "Last Frontier," home of many of North America's finest fish species and many of its great fly-fishing waters.

I had to admit: it had been quite a year for me – everything from fly-fishing saltwater for halibut and ling cod to flying out to the wilds of Alaska on several occasions, "chasing rainbows," experiencing all I could of Alaska's best rivers and its many fly rod species.

But more than anything else, I knew, the memory of the people I'd come to know in my travels – Alaska's colorful characters as they're called – would sustain me through the coming winter until the streams would begin to flow again and once more, like countless other flyfishers, I would beckon to the call of the river.

Chapter #15

Alaska Fishing Lodges & Services
-In Order of the Chapters-

- **The Charter Connection**
  Captain Jimmy Seas
  Seward, Alaska
  1-800-478-4446
  (907) 224-4446

- **Iliamna Lake Resort****
  Hosts: Masao Kikuchi, Jim Winchester
  P.O. Box 208 • Iliamna, Alaska 99606
  Ph: 907-571-1387   Fax: 907-571-1430

- **Bob Cusack's Alaska Lodge**
  Bob Cusack, Owner
  8920 SE 45th Street
  Mercer Island, Washington 98040
  206-232-3278
  907-571-1202 (Lodge)

- **Iliamna Bear Foot Adventures**
  Greg and Sally Hamm, Owners
  c/o P.O. Box 1146
  Willow, Alaska 99688
  907-563-2909 or 907-495-6388

- **Copper River Lodge**
  Dennis and Sharon McCracken
  P.O. Box 200831, Anchorage, Ak. 99520
  907-344-3677

- **Tony Sarp's KATMAI LODGE**
  Tony Sarp, Owner • Les Jacober, Manager
  2825 90th S.E. Everett, Washington 98204
  206-337-0326 Everett, Wash.
  Lodge: 907-439-3081 Alagnak River

- **Wood River Lodge - Tikchik Lakes**
  John and Linda Ortman
  Bernie and John Ortman, Jr.
  P.O. Box 997
  Whitefish, Montana 59937
  406-862-2305
  907-842-5200 (Lodge)

- **Mark, Greg, and Sandy Bell**
  High Adventure Air
  P.O. Box 486
  Soldotna, Alaska 99669
  907-262-7333

- **Bob Cusack's Alaska Lodge**
  Bob Cusack, Owner
  8920 SE 45th Street
  Mercer Island, Washington 98040
  206-232-3278
  907-571-1202 (Lodge)

- *Iliaska* Lodge, Lake Iliamna
  Ted and Mary Gerken, Owners
  6160 Farpoint Drive, Anch. Ak. 99507
  907-337-9844 Anchorage
  907-571-1221 (Iliamna)

- **Talarik Creek Lodge**
  Iliamna, Alaska
  Bruce Johnson, Manager
  907-571-1325 (Iliamna)
  208-263-8594

- **TalStar Lodge - Talachulitna River**
  Claire Dubin, Mike Patton
  P.O. Box 870978
  Wasilla, Alaska 99687
  June-September: 907-733-1672
  October - May: 907-688-1116

- **Ketchum Air Service**
  Craig Ketchum, Owner
  Based at Lake Hood, Anchorage
  Box 190588, Anchorage, Ak. 99519
  907-243-5525

- **Alaska TROUTFITTERS**
  Bob & Curt Trout, Owners
  2201 E. Parks Highway
  Wasilla, Alaska
  or Mile 50, Sterling Highway,
  Cooper Landing, Alaska
  907-595-1557 (Wasilla)
  907-376-7098 (Cooper Landing)

- Katmailand, Incorporated
  Raymond F. 'Sonny' Petersen, Owner
  - •Brooks Lodge
  - •Kulik Lodge
  - •Grosvenor Lodge
  4700 Aircraft Drive, Anchorage, Alaska 99502
  907-243-5448

- Alaska TROUTFITTERS
  Bob & Curt Trout, Owners
  2201 E. Parks Highway
  Wasilla, Alaska
  or Mile 50, Sterling Highway,
  Cooper Landing, Alaska
  907-595-1557 (Wasilla)
  907-376-7098 (Cooper Landing)

- Quinnat Landing Hotel
  King Salmon, Alaska
  Nanci Morris, Head Guide
  5520 Lake Otis Parkway
  Anchorage, Alaska 99507
  907-561-2310   Anchorage
  907-246-3000   King Salmon

- ILIAMNA AIRPORT HOTEL
  Lem Batchelder, Owner
  Hotel, Restaurant, Air Taxi, Hunting, Fishing
  P.O. Box 157, Iliamna, Alaska 99606
  907-571-1276

** Check on status of current operation

Chapter #16

Alaska's Salmon Species
Average and Record Weights

Here are typical and record weights for the five species of Alaska's pacific salmon:

1) <u>King Salmon</u>:   Rng: 15 -90 lbs. Avg: 35 lbs. Record: 97.4 lbs.
2) <u>Chum Salmon</u>: Rng: 7-17 lbs. Avg: 11 lbs. Record: 32.0 lbs.
3) <u>Red Salmon</u>:   Rng: 7-14 lbs. Avg: 9 lbs. Record 16.0 lbs.
4) <u>Pink Salmon</u>:   Rng: 3 -6 lbs. Avg: 4 lbs. Record 12.9 lbs.
5) <u>Silver Salmon</u>: Rng: 9-19 lbs. Avg: 12 lbs. Record 26.0 lbs.

Chapter #17

Alaska's Premier Waters
And Their Fish Species

Here is my list of many of Alaska's best rivers and fisheries, according to what I have experienced firsthand and from what I have learned from others. It should be noted that a handful of Alaska's smaller, premier fisheries have been omitted – simply because some of these unnamed rivers and streams are simply too small and fragile to survive an onslaught of fishing pressure.

Number Key For Individual Fish Species:

(1) Rainbow Trout (2) Steelhead (3) King Salmon
(4) Chum Salmon (5) Sockeyes (6) Silver Salmon
(7) Pink Salmon (8) Dollies/char (9) Lake Trout
(10) Arctic Grayling (11) Sheefish (12) Northern Pike
(13) Cutthroat

Agulukpak River 1-5-8-10
Agulowok River 1-3-4-5-6-7-8-10
Alagnak River (*Branch) 1-3-4-5-6-7-8-10
Aleknegik Lake 1-3-4-5-6-7-8-10-12
Alexander Creek 1-3-4-5-6-7-8-10
American Creek 1-5-8
Anchor River 1-2-3-6-7-8
Aniak River 1-3-4-6-7-8-10
Branch River (*Alagnak) 1-3-4-5-6-7-8-10
Brooks River 1-5-6-8-10
Buskin River (Kdk) 6-7-8
Chatanika River 7-8-10
Chilikadrotna River 1-3-4-5-6-7-8-10
Chuitna River (Chuit) 1-3-6-7-8
Clear Creek 1-3-6-7-10
Copper River (LI) 1-5-8-10
Council River 4-6-7-8-10-12
Crescent Lake 1-8-10
Deep Creek 1-2-3-6-7-8
Dream Creek 1-5-8-10
Fish River (WM) 3-4-6-7-8-10-12
Frazer River (Kdk) 2-5-6-8
Gibraltar River 1-5-8

Goodnews River (W) 1-3-4-5-6-7-8-10
Gulkana River 1-2-3-5-6-7-8
Holitna River 3-4-6-7-8-10-(11)
Iliamna River 1-5-8
Kakhonak River 1-5-8-10
Kamishak River 3-4-6-7-8-10
Kanektok River (West) 1-3-4-5-6-7-8-10
Karluk River (Kdk) 2-3-6-7-8
Karta River 2-5-6-7-8-13
Kenai Lake (Outlet) 1-3-5-6-7-8
Kenai River 1-3-5-6-7-8
Kisaralik River 1-3-4-6-7-8-10
Klawock River 1-2-6 + Salt
Kobuk River 4-8-10-(11)-12
Koktuli River 1-3-4-5-6-7-8-10
Koyuk River 3-4-6-7-8-10
Kukaklek Lake 1-4-5-6-7-8-9-10
Kulik River 1-5-6-8-10
Kvichak River 1-3-4-5-6-7-8-10
Lake Creek 1-3-4-5-6-7-8-10
Lewis Creek 1-3-4-6-7-8
Lake Louise 9-10
Little Willow 3-5-7-10
Minto Flats 10-12
Mulchatna River 1-3-4-5-6-7-8-10
Naknek River 1-3-4-5-6-7-8-10
Naknek Lake 1-3-5-6-7-9-10-12
Newhalen River 1-5-8-9-10
Nerka Lake 1-5-6-8-9-10-12
Ninilchik River 1-2-3-6-7-8
Nome River 6-7-10
Nonvianuk Lake 1-4-5-6-7-8-9-10
North River 3-4-6-7-8-10
Nushagak River 1-3-4-5-6-7-8-10
Nuyakuk River 1-5-8-10
Nuyakuk Lake 1-5-8-10

Russian River 1-3-5-8
Selawik River (N) 4-8-(11)-12
Sheep Creek 1-3-6-7-8
Situk River 2-3-6-8
Skilak Lake 1-3-5-6-7-8-9
Swanson River Systm. 1-8
Talachulitna River 1-3-4-5-6-7-8-10
Talkeetna River 1-3-4-6-7-8-10
Talarik Creek , Lower 1-5-8
Theodore 1-3-6-7-8-10
Thorne River (PWI) 2-4-6-7-8-13
Tikchik Lake 1-8-9-10
Tazimina River 1-5-10
Togiak River 1-3-4-5-6-7-8-10
Uganik River (Kdk) 2-3-5-6-7-8
Ugashik Narrows 5-6-8-10
Unalakleet River 3-4-6-7-8-10
Willow Creek 1-3-6-7-8
Wulik River 4-8-10